On The Rocks

On The Rocks
A lightkeeper's tale

Lawrence Tulloch

The Shetland Times Ltd.
Lerwick
2009

On The Rocks – A lightkeeper's tale

Printed and published by
The Shetland Times Ltd.,
Gremista, Lerwick,
Shetland ZE1 0PX.

CONTENTS

Continued on next page

CONTENTS CONTINUED

ILLUSTRATIONS

FOREWORD

I am delighted to write a foreword to this very necessary book about the life and times of a typical lightkeeper whose service covered some of the last years of manned lighthouses in Scotland. It is very necessary because relatively little is written about, or by, the dedicated men who spent their working lives in a rather strange, sometimes dangerous but often beautiful environment. It is also clear from this account that, for some at least, it was a very satisfying and fulfilling calling which was not without an element of fun and mischief to brighten an otherwise routine and regimented life.

The lighthouse service and its highly disciplined regime, so necessary to ensure unfailing availability of utterly reliable navigational aids, always appealed to a certain type of individual and such men were highly valued by the Northern Lighthouse Board. Many lightkeepers were drawn from the remote communities which played host to large and iconic lighthouses and in these areas good, secure and long-term employment was hard to find. This combination, together with an upbringing in close-knit family units produced men of the right character and temperament to be able to live the life demanded by the service. Their commitment is not often celebrated or documented so this record is especially valuable before time erases memory and we lose access to first-hand and vivid accounts of life in the lighthouse service. Apart from this the diary of ordinary daily life as a lighthouse-keeper is particularly fascinating the further it is left astern and we should treasure these fast-fading insights into the social history of the remote areas of Scotland.

This book, perhaps a little unwittingly, also pays tribute to the range of talents and skills required of a properly rounded and competent lightkeeper. The technical skills were wide-ranging enough for men with limited engineering knowledge, or formal training, but the requirement for social and domestic skills to make life congenial and comfortable on the station was equally formidable. The good humour and tolerance required is a strong thread running throughout this account and it is little wonder that life-long friendships were forged on those lonely outposts.

It is also very satisfying to find that most of the lightkeepers found the board to be a very good employer. The board has always sought to be so and its own record can support that. But perception is as important as reality and when both history and memory is long there is scope for at least misunderstanding. None is apparent here and this lightkeeper clearly looks back at his service as a period of cherished memory.

Finally to those of us who spent some of the happiest and most satisfying years of our lives at sea the unfailing reliability of the lighthouse services worldwide was an enormous comfort. Before electronic navigation – and that wasn't very long ago – the loom of a landfall light was welcome confirmation of dead-reckoning, combined with days of astro-navigation fixes, and sometimes none.

I'm glad that this book has been written. There are many similar stories to be told, but this will stand as a tribute to the life and times of the lightkeepers who contributed so much to the mission of the Northern Lighthouse Board to provide a service *In Salutem Omnium* – 'For the Safety of All'.

Capt. G. H. Sutherland FNI
Chairman, Northern Lighthouse Board, 2007-2009

ACKNOWLEDGEMENTS

It was not that long after I left the lighthouse service that I decided that I wanted to write a book about my time in it. It has been a long, drawn out, process and would have taken even longer, and might even have been impossible, but for the help of a number of people.

It is often said that writing is a lonely business and that is true insofar as any writer who sits at a keyboard usually does so in solitude. In this case I had, in my head, the company of so many friends and workmates associated with lighthouses, memories of them are fresh in my mind even after thirty odd years.

I thank the Northern Lighthouse Board for giving me a career in the service, a period that I look back on as the time of my life. The NLB was a wonderful employer; I doubt that their like still exists.

Being in the service was like being part of a big family, in it I felt cocooned and secure, and the circle was widened by the folk that lived on small islands and in rural villages, they welcomed, with open arms, lightkeepers and their families into their communities.

I think of all the established lightkeepers and their wives who helped me during my time as a supernumerary. Often it was a case of ships that passed in the night; we would meet up once only before I moved on to yet another station.

Captain George Sutherland kindly agreed to write a foreword for the book. At the time he was chairman of the Northern Lighthouse Board. The yawning gulf between the commissioners and ordinary lightkeepers was so wide that I hesitated, I thought long and hard, before I contacted him. In fact he was entirely approachable, he seemed to find it a little strange that I might think otherwise. Captain Sutherland is the only native Shetlander to serve as a commissioner, let alone chairman. His foreword shows great insight and it is a superb enhancement to *On the Rocks*.

Sincere thanks to Charlotte Black of *The Shetland Times* for so readily agreeing to publish it and to Brian Johnston for his work on the photos; also to Vaila Wishart for lending her expertise to correct my many errors and providing the most valuable advice.

Thanks to Tommy Budge for reading my efforts and to his wife Thelma and the entire Budge family for being the very best of friends and neighbours, and to all the other families who were our neighbours at Cape Wrath and Muckle Flugga.

Thanks to Jonathan Wills, in our early days at Muckle Flugga, for all his kindness and help. And, right now, thanks to him for so freely providing brilliant photos from our Flugga days. I am equally grateful to Anna Henderson of Skerries for lending precious irreplaceable photos, some of her late husband, Donnie. Thanks also to Dave Wheeler and Kieran Murray for allowing the use of their photos.

To our close family friend Alexa Fitzgibbon from France, thanks for the photo of me that appears on the back cover. It was taken at a concert in Fetlar when I was listening to one of my favourite Irish fiddle players. Sincere thanks to all the photographers who have enhanced *On the Rocks* with the images that bring the whole thing to life.

I thank, in advance, the tolerance of fellow lightkeepers who may recognise themselves on some of the pages. I have altered a few names to avoid embarrassment but I know that they can accept the tales in the same spirit as they were written. I could have written many more!

The biggest thanks of all has to go to my wife, Margaret. Without a single word of reservation she sacrificed her own career to be at my side and offered unfailing support no matter where my lightkeeping duties took me. She has also been great source information; often her memory is better than mine.

Lawrence Tulloch
November 2009

Chapter 1

Edinburgh Rock

IN THE summer of 1971 I found myself unemployed for the first time in my life. I was engaged to be married and to have an income and a home was essential, so I decided I must make an effort to find a proper and secure job.

I had been without a job all the previous winter. The only work I had done was as a Census enumerator. It had lasted just a short time but had landed me in trouble with the employment office, which accused me of claiming benefit to which I was not entitled. After months of argument and weeks without any benefit at all, I eventually won my case at a tribunal.

For a long time I had been interested in lighthouses. I had previously seen an advert in the situations vacant column of *The Shetland Times* stating that the Northern Lighthouse Board was looking for new lightkeepers. At the time I had thought of applying and now, I reckoned, I would take the plunge. As it turned out this was not so easy. The paper had been thrown out and I did not have a clue where to apply. My friends at the dole office could not help either. They did not know if the board needed more men at that time and they did not have the address. Eventually I obtained the necessary information and sent in an application.

On a bright breezy day in mid-May my father and I were cutting peats in the Head of Gutcher near our family home in Yell. When we went home in the middle of the day for dinner my mother told me there had been a phone call from the lighthouse board. This was an exciting piece of news. I had been waiting for such a call for weeks.

When I phoned back I spoke to a Mr Dickson. I was to have a lot of dealings with him in the years to come. He told me to report to Mr A. Scott Tulloch, the principal lightkeeper at Muckle Flugga, for a preliminary interview. This I did. Alex was, from the start, supportive of my application and as a result of his phone call to headquarters I was sent to the next stage, a medical report from my own doctor. This hurdle was overcome and I was summoned to appear in Edinburgh to be interviewed for a job.

On hearing this my father was sure that the rigours of the peat hill were my best chance of making a favourable impression in Edinburgh.

"Da sun an da wind ill pit a skeen apo de," he declared.

The lighthouse board's address is quite famous. It is 84 George Street, but at this time HQ was undergoing a major facelift and the temporary offices were at 28 North Bridge. Not that it made any difference to me. I would have been equally scared and nervous regardless of the locality.

I arrived promptly at 10am and what followed was a day I shall never forget. Mr Dickson, who proved to be younger than I expected, interviewed me. He was, perhaps, more or less my own age. I was given a written exam. Nothing too taxing, but I had to prove that I could read, write and solve arithmetical problems. For example, in a room 11 feet by 9, how many 9 inch square tiles would it take to cover the floor? And there were questions about costing meals for three men for a month's stay on a rock station.

I felt I had done well in all this and believed I had been accepted when I was sent to the board's tailors in George Street to be measured for uniform. This done, my next port of call was to Jerome's in Leith Walk to have passport photographs taken. The medical came next. The doctor I had to see had his surgery on the south side of the city, so much so that any further south was green fields. The medical was very thorough. This august gentleman of medicine, as they say, left no stone unturned and no avenue unexplored.

He was somewhat tight-lipped about the whole thing but I got the impression that while it was a damned close-run thing I had, nonetheless, rounded a nasty corner. I made my way back to 28 North Bridge in two minds. I was wondering if lightkeeping was all it was cracked up to be.

The news was in no way encouraging. I fully expected, after all I had been through, to be told I had been accepted. Not at all. My main interview was yet to come. The board secretary, Mr Welsh, gave me a friendly but thorough questioning. Gradually I began to understand the purpose of all the palaver. It was vitally important, from their point of view, to reject anyone who would not make a good lightkeeper. Given that men were thrown together and cooped up in lighthouses for a month at a time, they needed men who were tolerant, adaptable and resourceful. If an interview day taxed a would-be recruit to the limit, so much the better.

At the end of the interview with Mr Welsh I was pretty much a spent force, but my ordeal was to continue I was now told to write an essay about what I thought life would be like on a rock station. The fact that I had never been on a rock did not help but I did the best I could and seemed to get past that too.

By this time my patience was exhausted as well as being exhausted in general, so I asked the big question: "Have I been accepted?"

I got no straight answer but instead was told that I had to be interviewed by Mr Malcolm. Within the light board he was the biggest of big wheels but, although I did not know it, the fact that I had got this far meant that I was no more than a yard from the finishing line.

Among other, as I saw it, silly questions, Mr Malcolm asked if my glasses would blow off in a gale at a rock station. He told me several times that lighthouses were situated in remote places and that I, and my family, had to able to tolerate that. He did seem to appreciate that my fiancée and myself belonged to a very rural area and this was a plus.

Mr Malcolm was seeking to make doubly sure that I did not join the service to be disappointed and leave again at an early date. In the end he was satisfied. I was left in the room by myself and had to wait some time before Mr Dickson reappeared.

He told me that I had been accepted and that I would be paid as a supernumerary lightkeeper from the day that I left home. After all the stress of the day I think that if I had been rejected I would probably done Mr Dickson a serious mischief. Even now there were several formalities to complete. I had to sign the Official Secrets Act. The fact I had worked for the Post Office and signed the Act years ago cut no ice with Mr Dickson. I was issued with a first aid guide and a *Brown's Guide to Signalling*. I was paid the expenses I had incurred since leaving home and instructed how to claim expenses in the future.

I was told to pick up an air ticket, proceed to Sumburgh Head and report to the principal lightkeeper there, Mr Eddie Black. Finally, I was to go back to the photographers in Leith Walk and collect the passport photos taken earlier in the day. It was now late in the afternoon, so I was told to put them through the letterbox on the front door of NLB HQ.

The relief of being free of Mr Dickson and his colleagues was mighty and I went in search of a meal, a dram and an early bed. I suppose I should have been elated that I had gained my objective but I was so shell-shocked I just felt numb. Nonetheless, I had now joined the lighthouse service. It was 26th May, 1971.

CHAPTER 2

A TIME TO REFLECT

LATER that same night I sat in a bar near the bed and breakfast where I was staying, with a pint at my elbow, and took the opportunity to think about the day's doings and what led up to it.

I left school at the age of fifteen with no qualifications whatsoever, not even one O level. I had failed my 11-plus and finished my formal education at the Mid Yell Junior High School without much sense of purpose or direction.

I had been born in the north of the island of Yell, in Cullivoe. My father, Tom Tulloch, was a crofter, a woodworker and builder. Neither he nor my mother, Lisa, had ever had any higher education. They assumed that I would be content, as they were, to stay at home and live the traditional life, a life that offered little opportunity of betterment.

They never saw education as much of an asset and never encouraged me to strive and do well at school. It is not the case that I point any finger of blame towards them. I had in my own hands the opportunity but never tried to take it.

I had thought of trying to gain entry to Leith Nautical College. I had a notion that I would like to be a radio operator and toyed with the idea of joining the Royal Navy. In the event

Peter Spence, the sub-postmaster at Gutcher, offered me a job the day I left school, so I took it.

At that time jobs were hard to come by in Yell so I felt grateful to him. As well as running the post office he also had the telephone exchange and was a weaver and printer. He paid me the princely sum of £2 a week and taught me to do all those different things.

After I had been working for him for two years he resigned and went to live in Lerwick. My father was appointed sub-postmaster in his place but the telephone exchange was automated and it became abundantly clear that there was insufficient work for us all so I was adrift again without a rudder.

As luck would have it I was soon offered another job, as a machine knitter. Dr Harry Nisbet, an Edinburgh man with strong Yell connections, planned to set up a knitwear unit and I was given the chance of training on hand flat machines in Tillicoultry, Clackmannanshire. I spent a lot of time away from home and, by and large, my time working in knitwear factories was happy. I made many good friends both at home and in Scotland. However, one of the first lessons learned in the knitwear business was that there were good times and bad times and the good times never quite made up for the bad. In the end the whole thing petered out and, in any case, I was acutely aware that working as a machine knitter was not something for the long term.

At a wedding in the Sellafirth hall I met the love of my life. She was someone I had known all her life but had never seen as a girlfriend or someone to fall in love with. I took Margaret Henderson home to Gloup from the wedding and we have been a couple ever since, and ever since she has been, by far and away, the most important person in my life. The only other one who is upsides with her is our daughter Liz. I am eight years older than Margaret but she is a lot more clever. She went to the Anderson High School in Lerwick so we were never at school together, despite the fact that we were born within two miles of each other.

For the first time in my life I had a real purpose and a real aim. I wanted to marry Margaret and the need for a proper job was imperative. To drift along taking whatever was offered was no longer an option. She went to college in Aberdeen, Robert Gordon's, taking a three-year course in institutional management. She had already agreed to marry me but it could not be until she finished college.

Becoming a lightkeeper solved all my problems of employment and housing. Margaret and I spent most of our courtship apart but our commitment to each other never wavered so on that May night in Edinburgh I had ample food for thought. Uppermost in my mind were the questions: "Have I bitten off more than I can chew? Can I do this job? Can I work at heights? Will Margaret be happy with life in the lighthouse service?"

I had been asked several times during my interviews if I could work at heights and I had said yes. They never asked if I was frightened of heights. The answer to that question was a very definite yes, but being frightened and being able to do it were two different things.

Whatever my misgivings, the future looked bright and exciting and at the age of twenty-eight I felt my life was only just beginning. I made myself a silent promise that it really was a new start and I would give it my very best shot. I could hardly wait to tell Margaret and my parents the good news.

CHAPTER 3

SUMBURGH HEAD

WHEN I arrived at Sumburgh Airport the following day I was met by Eddie Black. Eddie was a small, grey-haired man who looked old to me. I had no difficulty in knowing who he was because he was wearing a lighthouse uniform over a heavy white polo necked jumper.

He was very friendly and talked a lot as we drove up the narrow winding road that leads to the lighthouse. He invited me into his house where his wife, Georgie, had the kettle on and soon I was drinking tea and eating biscuits. In the course of conversation Georgie mentioned that her knitting machine was giving her trouble. When I said I was used to working on knitting machines she asked if I would be so good as to check out hers. It proved to be no more than a needle with a dodgy latch so I fixed that and also made a few adjustments to the thread carriers. So my first job, in my new career, had nothing to do with lighthouses.

The machine fixed and the tea and biscuits consumed, I was shown my quarters, my home, for the time being. Every lighthouse had a bothy, usually a single room with two bunk beds, two chairs, a table and a small cooker. The bothy at Sumburgh was, I learned, typical. Any supernumerary or

occasional keeper lived, ate and slept in the bothy. While it was warm and fairly comfortable it was no more than the most basic accommodation. If two men were sharing there was no privacy and food had to be shared because of the lack of cooking space.

Sharing the bothy with me at Sumburgh was Andy Flaws from Skelberry in Dunrossness. He was the occasional lightkeeper. Andy was a pleasant companion. He had been, in his younger days, a ship's officer and had many interesting stories to tell. However, the bad times he had experienced during World War Two still troubled him. He suffered really bad nightmares and the first time I was aware of this he scared the living daylights out of me. I had come off watch at 2am and climbed into the upper bunk. I was in that lovely twilight zone, nearly asleep, when Andy roared like a bull and punched the bottom of my bed until I quite literally hit the ceiling with my head. I was hardly best pleased and leaned over the edge of the bed to ask him what the hell he thought he was doing but it was no use, he was sound asleep and never knew he had done such a thing. After this, even if I never got used to his disturbed sleep, at least I knew to expect it.

On my first full day at work I met the other lightkeepers, Jimmy Watt and Robbie Sinclair. It was because Robbie had resigned from the service that I was there. He was starting a new venture, a laundry in Lerwick, and I was to be relief for him when he had finished working his notice.

For my first two weeks I was to be Eddie's shadow. I shared his watches and he taught me all the things I needed to know before being given the responsibility of going on watch by myself. During this time he gave me a wealth of information

Andy Flaws in the Sumburgh lighthouse. © *Shetland Museum and Archives*

about the job and what was expected of every lightkeeper. He told me I was on probation and sent a report on my progress to HQ at regular intervals. Any lapse of duty invited instant dismissal. However, diligent Supers were valued highly by the management. It was not just Supers that had to do their duty. Any keeper, no matter how senior, would be sacked for neglect of duty.

The main duty was the light. It was of paramount importance that the light worked to maximum efficiency during the hours of darkness. The light at Sumburgh Head ran on paraffin. It was a pressure lamp with an 85mm mantle. The paraffin was forced through a vaporiser and the resulting gas burned in the mantle producing a brilliant light. The light was magnified a thousand-fold by the lens through which it shone. The lens was two and a half tons of precisely ground glass that revolved floating on a bed of mercury. It would move, despite its weight, at the touch of one finger. It was driven by a giant clockwork motor in exactly the same way as a grandfather clock. In a lighthouse the weight went down through the centre of the tower and the staircase spiralled around it. Like any other clock it had to be wound up; in the case of Sumburgh every forty minutes.

The light had a character of three white flashes every thirty seconds so it was equally important that the lens turned at the correct speed. The speed was regulated by brass plates that revolved fast and they could be set side-on or edge-on to the air. As well as winding up the clockwork motor the paraffin tank had to be pumped, with a double foot pump, to keep forcing the

Sumburgh Head. © Kieran Murray

oil to the lamp. There was always a second lamp ready for use if the lamp being used developed any problem.

A big factor at Sumburgh Head was fog. It is an area very prone to low cloud and sea fog. Whenever the visibility dropped below a certain critical level the fog signal had to be sounded. Landmarks along the coastline were used in making the decision as to whether the foghorn had to be sounded

I was impressed by everything at the station but was mighty impressed by the engine room. It contained three huge engines, 44hp Kelvin diesels that drove the air compressors that powered the sirens. Two of those engines were on load, in times of fog, with the third on standby. After the engines were started up they were allowed to run until the pressure built up and then a series of valves were opened to allow the compressed air into the siren. Then all hell broke loose. The noise of the foghorn was loud beyond belief, designed to be heard many miles away.

Maybe the most impressive aspect of the engine room was its cleanliness. It was immaculate, with a tiled floor that you could eat your dinner off and the engines were a mass of polished, gleaming copper and brass. Nowhere was there a speck of dust or dirt. It took much time and no little elbow grease to keep it like that.

CHAPTER 4

LIFE AS A SUPER

THE first two weeks were looked on as basic training and prepared me for the time when I would keep a watch by myself. Each night watch lasted four hours, from 6pm to 10pm, from 10pm until 2am and from 2am until 6am. The man who had done the 6pm to 10pm watch was back on at 6am. Six-hour watches were kept during the day so that the watches rotated, otherwise each keeper would have the same night watches all the time. Each man was entitled to a day off every week and this is where the occasional lightkeeper, Andy Flaws, came in.

I had only been there for three days when Eddie asked me the big question, the question I knew I had to answer but the one I dreaded nonetheless. "Can you work at heights?"

I told him I was frightened of heights but had never had to work off the ground so did not know the answer. He told me in a kindly but firm way that if I could not work at heights I had no future as a lightkeeper. He went on to say that we would paint the dome of the lighthouse that very day. I suppose that I was in some ways relieved that I was to be put to the test. The issue had to be resolved so I might as well get it over with.

Jimmy Watt and I got paint, paint brushes and rigged on safety belts and climbed to the top of the lighthouse and out on to the balcony. I had no fear of the height on the balcony because a high railing ensured it was entirely safe. Above that it was a different story. A short iron ladder led to the dome. Jimmy climbed it first and I followed with white knuckles and pounding heart. A narrow guttering was all we had to stand on and I was so nervous that I had great difficulty fastening my safety belt. An aircraft came in over the top of us and looked disconcertingly near. We had worked our way to the far side, away from the ladder, and began to paint. I was far from being either comfortable or relaxed and I knew my painting was sloppy, but I also knew I was not going to be thrown out of the service because of the heights issue.

So focused was I that I never looked down, or anywhere else for that matter, so I was unaware of Eddie. He was on the dome too. It was not that he had any intention of painting. He had on uniform trousers, a gansey and carpet slippers. He had come to see how I was getting on, to tell some dubious jokes, and tell us both to come down because it was coffee time.

It felt good to be back on the earth again and the relief, the knowledge that I could work on the dome, was stupendous. However, I had another harsh lesson to learn. When the coffee break was over we had to go back up to finish the job. Going up the first time was hard but going up the second was ten times worse. I had steeled myself to go but now the adrenalin was spent and I was more nervous than ever. Somehow I got through and both Eddie and Jimmy congratulated me on overcoming my fear and being able to do a job at the top of the lighthouse. I never told them that I had not conquered my fear of heights and I never did overcome that fear but I knew I could do it when I had to. In all the rest of my time as a lightkeeper if

I had to work high I made sure I never came down until the job was finished. For me it was a case of aye the langer aye the waur.

Robbie Sinclair packed up his belongings and left the station for the last time and this was highly important for me in two ways. First of all Eddie told me that from now on I would keep a watch by myself and that if I wanted I could move into the empty house vacated by Robbie. To be on watch by myself was hugely exciting and I felt a great sense of responsibility but it was midsummer and the light was not shown for a very long period. A large wallboard gave lighting up and extinguishing times for the whole year and this was followed to the minute. Lighting up time could be brought forward by 30 minutes if the sky was very dark.

I had strict instructions from Eddie that I was to call him if I got into any difficulties. I felt that to call him out in the middle of the night would be a last resort because I should be able to manage, having been shown how to do everything. I had moments of indecision but managed to complete the watch without any major incident.

The highlight of my stay at Sumburgh was when Margaret came to visit. I had a house all to myself and we were engaged to be married but nonetheless, in those days, any unmarried couple had to spend unchaperoned time with discretion. To overcome that hurdle Jimmy and Liz Watt "invited" Margaret to stay with them. Of course she stayed with me but would spend a lot of time with Liz and, needless to say, it was not long before Andy arrived to run an eye over "yon lass a dine". If he had been aware of the domestic arrangements he would have disapproved most strongly. On the other hand I think that Eddie knew but turned a blind eye.

For me it was a delightful weekend but was gone all too soon. Margaret was off to London as part of her course. She was to work in the kitchens of the Shell Centre. We were used to being apart and quickly settled down again to the usual routine of phone calls and love letters.

The next big event at the lighthouse was the annual inspection. The inspection was carried out by the NLB superintendent, Mr Smith. Most lightkeepers dreaded the inspection because they came under intense scrutiny. Mr Smith and his assistants were all promoted from being engineers on lighthouse ships. The purpose of the annual visit was to see that the station was run and maintained properly. Superintendents would go into the lightkeepers' houses and check that they were kept clean and in good order. Some would go as far as to wear white gloves and run a finger along a door top or above a facing to check that it had been dusted.

Mr Smith was a confirmed bachelor and it was said he was uncomfortable in the company of women so he was always reluctant to venture into the houses. Lightkeepers' wives were, to a woman, resentful of the suggestion that they were incapable or too lazy to do the housework, so it seemed that a state of armed truce existed between Mr Smith and the ladies.

A far more important aspect of an annual inspection was the discussion between the superintendent and the principal lightkeeper regarding the maintenance work needed at the station. Each summer was spent lime washing and re-painting the station. Some painting and tarring was done every year but other parts were done every other year or as needed.

The superintendent, at the end of the inspection, would write out a series of works orders. These were forms authorising a programme of jobs to be done. Works orders allowed lightkeepers to claim extra pay, as maintenance work was considered to be over and above normal lightkeeping duties. Of course keepers welcomed the works orders because the extra money came as something of a bonus. Any works order for inside work was especially welcome. That work was always kept for winter when work outdoors was impossible.

As it happened I was on watch during the time that Mr Smith was at Sumburgh Head. I adopted a policy of keeping well out of the way. A low profile seemed the wisest course of action. At first that worked well but banks of sea fog began to roll in and I knew that sooner rather than later I would have to start the foghorn. The fact that the visibility was getting worse by the minute had not escaped Mr Smith's sharp eye and I knew that the same sharp eye was going to watch, like a hawk, every move I made. Not a time to make a hash of things. I started the two engines and allowed them to build up air pressure. The valves that fed the air into the siren had to be opened in the correct order but fog was so common at Sumburgh that I had had quite a lot of practice already. The valves were opened and shut by means of a wheel about a foot in diameter mounted on a brass shaft. The cast iron wheels were so heavy that if they were spun fast they could twist off the brass shaft. It was here that I found the nerve to wind up Mr Smith, probably not one of my better ideas, but I spun the wheel really hard and slowed it with my other hand just as he had his mouth open to shout at me. Those wheels had to be turned in the same way as a learner driver is taught to turn the steering wheel of a car, with no crossing of the hands.

No-one was sorry when Mr Smith left the station. In fact there was a collective sigh of relief. He turned back briefly and spoke to me directly for the first time.

"Remember you will not be here all the time and remember every station is not as easy as this one."

Before I had time to reply he turned on his heel and marched out through the gate.

How right he was.

CHAPTER 5

ON THE MOVE

IT WAS only a few days later when the phone rang with news for me. It was Mr Dickson from the personnel department. I was to proceed to Muckle Flugga. Neither Eddie nor anyone else was surprised. I had been at Sumburgh Head for five weeks and that is quite a long time for a Super to be at any one station.

I packed up my gear and headed north to Unst. I was able to call in and see my parents in Gutcher. I had already phoned my Aunt Agnes and Uncle Peter to ask if I could stay with them overnight before going to the lighthouse. They stayed in Haroldswick, only a short distance from the shore station.

Muckle Flugga is the most northerly lighthouse in the British Isles. In fact only the Out Stack, a small barren lump of rock, is further north. It is entirely exposed and without shelter with the Arctic Ocean to the north, America to the west and Norway to the east. Many a time, especially in winter, landing by boat was impossible.

This was the middle of summer but, on the relief morning, no landing was possible. Communications were by radio. The lightkeeper on duty would talk to the boatman and the boat's crew and lightkeepers ashore would listen in on shortwave radio to hear the news.

The first "speak" was at 8am and on this occasion they were to review the situation at 2pm. At 2pm the sea conditions remained the same so the relief was called off for the day. We all listened in the following morning but still no landing was possible, and so it was for the next five days.

On the Sunday morning a landing was possible so we all gathered at the shore station and took all the stores for the lighthouse to the jetty. Travelling with me to the lighthouse was Jimmy Andrew Sinclair. He was the occasional lightkeeper and was to be on Muckle Flugga for the next four weeks.

Jimmy Lowry Edwardson was the skipper of the boat, the *Grace Darling,* and at retiring age he was about the youngest man on board. He had been on the boat for well over thirty years and had been made an MBE for his contribution to the lighthouse service. Not only that, but he had an unblemished record. Never in all that time did he even pick up a scratch on the *Grace Darling*.

I learned later that Lowry was famous for his lack of patience and tolerance. When the crew was called out he expected them to be at the shore station at once. He was heard to shout into the radio, when he called out the crew one beautiful, flat calm, summer morning: "Come you, boys. Come you as fast as you can. Der a gale warning fur Finisterre!"

Like everything else to do with lighthouses the boat was kept in apple pie order. It was as clean as a whistle and the varnish looked as if it been applied only yesterday. The smart appearance of the boat was helped by the fact that she was kept inside a boat shed. The geo at the shore station did not provide sufficient shelter for the boat either to lie at the pier or at

Muckle Flugga Shore Station. Photo by Lawrence Tulloch ➤

anchor. In a very smooth and well-practised operation the *Grace Darling* slid down the slipway and into the water and tied up alongside the small jetty. All the stores were loaded as well as the lightkeepers' boxes. Every keeper had a wooden box for clothes and personal effects.

Soon everything was onboard, including myself. The ropes were cast off and we were on our way to the rock, a huge adventure for me. At that stage I hardly knew any of the crew but it is true to say that they were, age-wise, in the veteran class. Indeed Willie Matthewson, "Peerie Willie", had been in the boat for over fifty years.

I had no way of knowing it at the time but those men, Johnny Charlie and Willie Gibby Mathieson, Peter Sinclair, Tammy Priest, Bertie Mathieson, Peerie Willie and Jimmy Lowry Edwardson himself, were to become my good friends and our lifeline to the shore. This crew had seen, in their time, every different situation that the weather conditions caused.

There was no hint, from any of them, about what they thought of the state of the sea or whether a landing would be possible. For my part I believed that if the boat was going to the rock then a landing was a certainty. This did not alter the fact that the Flugga Sound was rough, the canvas dodgers were raised and everyone cowered under them to avoid the plentiful spray that came inboard.

When the landing area came in sight the two lightkeepers going ashore were to be seen standing on the Comb with the mooring ropes at the ready. Jimmy Lowry was quick to express his doubts. With a profusion of oaths and expletives he questioned the sanity of anyone who was stupid enough to think that he was about to commit suicide.

However he went through what was to become a familiar routine. He put the *Grace Darling* in a wide circle that took us as close as he dared go to the Comb. The Comb at Muckle Flugga is a sort of natural pier but there is a baa a few yards from the point that has to be steered around when coming into the landing. The boat has to carry enough speed to allow proper steering but as soon as the Comb is reached a quick stop is vital otherwise the boat would crash into the rocks and ground. It all added up to a tricky operation and no matter how often it was done any complacency or lack of concentration could be fatal. The *Grace Darling* was far too heavy for the reverse gear to be effective. Even driving full astern made little difference, so the fastening of the massive stern rope quickly and securely was of paramount importance and this, too, was teamwork. The lightkeeper throwing the rope had to do so with exact timing and accuracy. Bertie Mathieson had to catch the flying heaving line with the skill of a slip fielder at cricket. To miss was unthinkable. The inevitable result would be grounding on the rocks or, if the rope missed the stern of the boat, probably a fouled propeller as well as grounding. It could be very difficult in strong winds and when the boat was pitching and rolling.

After making a number of circles Lowry had the situation sized up. In a voice like thunder he said we were going in for the landing and every man was to be ready. The final circle was much wider than any of the others but even so Lowry was not entirely satisfied with the way the boat aligned with the landing so he aborted the attempt. Yet another turn was performed and this time it was in earnest. When the *Grace Darling* was close to the landing and committed organised chaos reigned. Ropes flew through the air, men scrambled frantically to secure them while Lowry roared and swore like a madman remonstrating with a deaf and disobedient dog.

The all-important stern rope was made fast so the boat could go no further forward and two men hauled in the bow rope to prevent any surge backwards or forwards. Meanwhile the breast rope, the rope that stopped the boat from touching the rock abeam was likewise fastened. Thus the boat was securely tied and kept opposite the ladder up to the top of the Comb. But there was no hesitation. Lowry was roaring that we were to get a move on. I was unaware of the protocol but as the most junior man I was first to be landed. Almost before I knew what was happening a rope was put around my waist. After that I knew what I had to do. I climbed on to the gunwale. The rope I was tied to was suspended from a derrick and the two men still on the rock were taking in the slack. I then took hold of the rope with both hands and swung, Tarzan style, towards the iron ladder. The gap was not so wide, perhaps ten or twelve feet, but it was easy to turn around in mid-air with the danger of back injury if a man crashed into the ladder. To make sure this did not happen a lanyard, also fastened to me, was held by a boatman to slow down my swing.

As soon as I got hold of the ladder I was ordered to release the rope and as soon as I did it was fastened around the waist of Alex Scott Tulloch, the principal lightkeeper, who immediately launched himself towards the boat where he made a safe but less than dignified boarding. In a trice Jimmy Andrew was beside me on the rock and Rae Phillips was in the boat.

The reason for the order of who landed first and last was twofold. If for any reason the landing had to be abandoned the principal keeper was on the right side of things. It ensured that the senior men were where they wanted to be first. On the opposite relief, when the principal keeper was landing on the rock he would be the last man out of the boat. The other reason was that when a procedure was established there was no doubt in anyone's mind about how the relief proceeded. On a bad day there was no time to debate or argue about who was first in the queue.

While all this was going on the cargo was being loaded and unloaded. Muckle Flugga had a Blondin wire that stretched from the landing area to the top of the rock. As it happened the wire was at the perfect angle of 45 degrees; the distance and height was exactly right for this. Cargo was taken up and down this wire in the same way as a cable car works at a ski resort. Gravity took the load down but a motor-driven winch hauled it up again. The wire could bear a payload of 14cwt.

In a matter of seconds the mooring ropes were untied and the boat was on her way back to the shore leaving Jimmy Andrew and me feeling somewhat shell-shocked, standing watching the *Grace Darling* disappear around Sharp's Point. We now had the quite heavy task of securing and readying the ropes for next time there was a relief.

The bow and stern ropes were carefully coiled and hung on hooks concreted into the rock. The coils had to be a certain diameter so that the rope hung clear of the ground to avoid rubbing caused by heavy seas. The breast rope was pulled tight and tied to keep it high above the sea. When all this was done we began the climb up the 258 steps to the top of the rock.

CHAPTER 6

LIFE ON THE ROCK

THE third man on Flugga with us was Hugh Arthur. He was needed at the top during the relief to work the winch. Somewhat surprisingly it was Jimmy Andrew who was in charge and Hugh was to be the cook for the week ahead. Hugh was about the same age as myself but had been an appointed lightkeeper for a couple of years or so.

His first task that morning was to cook breakfast for Jimmy and I. We had bacon and eggs with fried bread, tea and toast. The next job was to put away the stores. Rock stations had a system of keeping emergency stores in case the relief went overdue. Anything in the emergency stores that could perish was used and replaced with fresh food. Muckle Flugga had three large deep freezes so food was plentiful and it would take many months without a relief before keepers would feel pangs of hunger. As I was to learn, each man at a rock station was given a daily allowance for food. In the event of workmen or artificers visiting the lightkeepers were entitled to charge them for their keep.

Spent wisely, the money for food was entirely adequate. In fact, sometimes there was a surplus. Meat and potatoes were bought in bulk locally and any extra money was used to buy luxuries. The lightkeepers had a friend who worked in the NAAFI shop in Haroldswick, part of the RAF presence in the island. The shop stocked numerous goods that were unavailable in local shops. They had a very attractive selection of bottled sauce, pickles and preserves. We also got catering-sized tins of coffee there.

My first and foremost task on Muckle Flugga was to learn enough about the station to be able to keep a watch on my own. At first it seemed very daunting, much more complicated than Sumburgh Head. The rock had no mains electricity but the light was, in fact, electric. This might seem strange but the lighthouse board never looked on the mains supply as reliable enough that it could be trusted not to fail. At Muckle Flugga there were four generators. The main generators were three Ruston-Hornsbys that had seen better days. They were run in rotation, one at a time with the other two on standby. More often than not they were overloaded. They were difficult to start and leaked oil and diesel. The fourth was a more modern Lister that was started each day just before lighting-up time. This provided power for the accommodation block, leaving more for the light itself.

The light was, in fact, two lights. The main light showed two white flashes every twenty seconds and was visible through 360 degrees. The second light was red, designed to warn of the danger of Lamba Ness, a headland on the north-east coast of Unst. Any ship steaming north along the east coast was in danger if they could see the red light. It had to change course and stay further away from the shore and Lamba Ness. The electric bulbs were, in each case, about nine inches in diameter. The white light had a 1000W bulb and the red light a 1500W bulb. The bulb holder was double so that if a bulb fused the

second bulb came on load immediately. An alarm was sounded and the keeper on watch would go and replace the dead lamp.

Muckle Flugga had a clockwork mechanism. It was much smaller but not unlike that of Sumburgh Head. No hand winding was necessary because there was an electric motor that automatically rewound the clockwork whenever it was needed. Muckle Flugga had no fog signal so visibility was never a concern for lightkeepers but there was a radio beacon. This transmitted a signal, in Morse code, that could be picked up in the radio room of a ship. By and large this needed no attention but the watchkeeper would monitor its performance on a regular basis. This was never difficult because such was the strength of the transmission that it was rather intrusive. It could be heard on all radio stations and on the TV. Each morning the clocks on the beacon were checked and set to the exact time with the pips on the national radio.

Strictly speaking, lightkeepers on watch were not allowed to leave the light room. In the case of Muckle Flugga the old, original kitchen, in the tower, was the official watch room. It was a comfortable place to keep watch. As the light revolved the watchkeeper could see the beam shining on the radio mast and the monitor for the radio beacon was on the wall. As in every other lighthouse, staying in the watch room all the time was not an option although on a bad night it was the best place to be. Engines had to be checked and the rules recognised this. It was known as a "wandering watch" and many a time a lightkeeper would do certain chores, like polishing brass or washing clothes when everyone else was in bed.

The author with Muckle Flugga and Out Stack in the background. Photo by David MacDonald

Muckle Flugga had a new accommodation block built in 1968 so each man had his own bedroom. I was given the principal's room and was delighted to find an electric blanket on the bed. Although it was midsummer it was cold and to slide into a warm bed at 2.30 in the morning was a real pleasure. The blanket, with thick, quality downies, made the beds comfortable indeed. The beds were built in and made from solid teak with wardrobes to match. There was also cupboard space and deep, wide drawers under the beds. The outer walls were of a double and a single brick, making two cavities and utmost weatherproofing.

Heavy sea at the landing. © Jonathan Wills

CHAPTER *7*

A STEEP LEARNING CURVE

IN THE next few days my head was bursting with the number of things I had to learn and remember. One of the more interesting things was the "speaks" on the radio. Three times a day Muckle Flugga, the shore station, Bressay and the Skerries spoke to each other on the radiotelephone. This took place at 8am, 2pm and 6.30pm. There was never a great deal to say but it gave reassurance that all was well. In the old days the keeper ashore from Muckle Flugga had to toil, rain or shine, to the top of Hermaness and exchange semaphore signals with the lighthouse. Radios had made life a lot easier.

On Sunday mornings we had test a call from the Coastguard in Lerwick on the distress frequency, 2182, but we did not linger there in case the channel was needed for real. As well as the main radio we had a VHF transmitter/receiver that could be linked to the telephone. This was a two-way system, unlike the conventional radio where transmitting and receiving could not be done simultaneously. The person transmitting, when speaking, had to press a button on the hand set and at the end of a transmission say "over" This was the signal for the other person to reply. The VHF had a Duplex system and, if it all worked well, a conversation could take place as in a telephone call. One drawback, with either radio, was the total lack of privacy. Any conversation could be listened to by anyone with a suitable receiver. And with the VHF someone had to link it in to the telephone.

At the shore station anyone linking the radio to the telephone always, tactfully, pretended not to hear what husbands and wives, boyfriends and girlfriends, were saying to each other. In fact it was difficult not to hear and if the speaker was switched on the whole conversion boomed out.

Very often, at the Muckle Flugga shore station, it was Lowry the boatman, who tended the radio hut. He had no inhibitions or scruples about listening to private conversations. For part of this time Margaret was at home in Gloup with her parents. For me it was a case of so near and yet so far. I spoke to her on the VHF every night and every time, without fail, Lowry would call me back to the radio.

"Boy whit wus yon it do wus sayin tae yon lass o dine? I didna fairly catch it."

A whole re-run of the conversation followed. Lowry was never satisfied until he got to the bottom of every last detail. We all knew the score so it was no big problem, more of a laugh.

For my first day or two Jimmy Andrew concentrated on teaching me about the light and watchkeeping but when he felt I had a grasp of that he showed me the station routine and where to find things. As well as the engine and radio room there was a paint store for paint and ropes. This was a building erected when the new accommodation block was built. It was a cookhouse then. At the back there was a small hut where the bottled gas was kept and there was also the smiddy. Maybe in the past it was used for metalworking but, in my time there, it was a workshop for doing any kind of woodwork. A quantity of wood was stored there. Mostly it belonged to lightkeepers who had woodworking for a hobby but Jimmy Andrew drew my attention to some broad white boards, new wood just as it came from a sawmill, and asked me if I knew what they were for. Needless to say I had no idea, so he explained that they were coffin boards. At first I thought he was winding me up but it was the case that all rock stations were supplied with enough suitable wood to make a coffin.

It seems that in the early days of lighthouses only two men manned some rocks. At one lighthouse the two keepers had a known history of bad blood between them. On shore leave if they met at the pub they sometimes came to blows and were heard to threaten to kill each other. It is odd that they were compelled to work together but they were. Near the start of a six-week stint on the lighthouse the older of the two died of natural causes. This put the other one in a serious fix. Not only did he have to do all the work by himself but he also felt certain he would be accused of murder. There was no question of any disposal of the corpse, like burial at sea. The body had to be examined by doctors as this was his only hope of vindication. Without any means of contacting the shore his plight was grim. To live in a cramped space with a decomposing corpse was more than he could endure. He fell on the plan of making a harness from rope, putting the dead man into it and hanging him on the wall outside. When the corpse was examined and no sign of injury was found his story was believed. Ever after that each lighthouse had a crew of three and wood for coffins became part of the stores.

The other two buildings on Muckle Flugga were the red light house and the winch house. The red light house was a small kiosk that contained a light that shone through a red lantern in the direction of Lamba Ness. The winch house was much more interesting, with the engine and winch that hauled up the cargo from the landing. There was considerable skill in driving the winch. To be reckless or careless was to risk breaking or damaging the main wire and there was also the danger of spilling and losing cargo or, worse still, crashing it all into the *Grace Darling*.

Hauling cargo up was fairly straightforward as long as it was stopped at the top but great care had to be taken when lowering cargo. One of the biggest problems was the braking system. It was very fierce. Any sudden stab with the foot and it all came to a shuddering halt, putting severe strain on everything.

I had a few practice runs and did not find it too difficult to learn but it was vital that any cargo had to be secured in the slings before hoisting or lowering was attempted. Badly prepared slings were big trouble and dangerous and anyone guilty incurred, from Lowry, the strongest verbal lambasting this formidable man could muster.

CHAPTER 8

FEEDING FIVE

FOR the second week it was my turn to be cook. I was very happy to cook for myself and even cooking for three was not too bad but two painters arrived so I had five to feed. Frank MacGregor and Willie Manson from Caithness had a summer contract to go around various lighthouses painting the tall masts that carried the aerials for the radio beacons.

Masts were anything up to a hundred feet high and the painting was looked on as a specialist job which lightkeepers were not asked to do. It was certainly difficult. To climb to the top was a task in itself and could only be done in calm weather. The masts were made from open angle irons bolted together and there was no such a thing as a lee side.

Frank and Willie had to wear safety belts and to paint the sections they had to brace their feet against a girder and lean back on the belt. This took a lot of nerve and I am so glad I was never asked to do anything like it. Although Frank and Willie were seasoned and experienced they still had to screw up their courage to go to the top.

To cook for four comparative strangers fully tested my nerve, albeit in a different way. The main meal every day was dinner, served at 1pm. The reason for this was that the middle of the day was the only time that no-one was in bed. Because of the watches during the night keepers often slept in the afternoons.

Dinner was always a two-course affair and it was entirely up to the cook what he served. Meals were, by and large, simple and wholesome and very, very adequate. As well as the fact that most keepers were moderately good cooks there was also the need to serve food that everyone could eat.

Beef and pork were bought in bulk from butchers and lamb was bought, whole carcases, locally, to be cut and portioned by the lightkeepers for storage in the deep freezes. While meat was plentiful fish was harder to obtain and when it came it was usually given by anyone who had fish going spare. All the scrappy cuts of meat were used to make stock for soup and popular among main courses was stew, mince, roasts and salt fish. We always had potatoes and whatever vegetables were available. Desserts varied. We had rice pudding, apple crumble, trifle, jelly, ice cream and on occasions plum duff.

On Sundays we nearly always had roast chicken and trimmings, and always on Sundays we had a sweet. Curry was also popular but the cook had to know that everyone liked spicy food. Tea was always high tea. Sausages, burgers and sassermaet were often served with chips and beans. The man on watch from 6pm till 10pm made the supper and this was, more often than not, any leftovers from dinner – cold meat, potatoes perhaps with bread, cheese and tea or coffee. If there were no leftovers there was always plenty of canned food, meat, sardines and pilchards. There was also pasta, rice and cereal. No-one went hungry on Muckle Flugga.

My first week of cooking went reasonably well but I did have a few scary moments. The first came when I had to mix milk. I had given no thought to where milk came from. I knew there was no source of fresh milk, and I knew that a big baking bowl of milk was kept in the fridge. Hugh Arthur showed me what had to be done. Milk came in powder form, its brand name was Millac. It had to be dissolved in water and beaten in with a whisk to avoid any lumps. A cup always floated in the milk as a means of filling a milk jug for the table.

My other scary moment, and this really was scary, was when I made macaroni cheese for tea one night. The trouble came when I put the tea in the teapot. There were no such things as tea bags at Muckle Flugga – the principal did not like them – and so it was all loose tea leaves. I was harassed and trying to do a number of different things at the same time. In any event, when I became aware of what I was doing I realised I was spooning tea leaves into the saucepan of macaroni and cheese. I tried to be calm, but I had no plan B. It was macaroni or nothing. There was plenty more macaroni in the cupboard but no time to boil it. The men would be in, looking for their tea, at any moment. Something had to be done and done quickly. I took a teaspoon and skimmed as much of the tea as I could from the macaroni but it was impossible to get it all out so I stirred in the rest. In an inspirational moment I told the men that the black specks in the cheese sauce, if they wondered what they were, were herbs that I had added for extra flavour. It was all eaten and nobody passed any remark so I was mighty relieved and wiped a troubled brow.

All week I was in the kitchen I played safe. I worked within my limits and cooked low-risk meals. As cook I was responsible for keeping the kitchen clean and washing the dishes but it was the custom for someone to stay and dry. At the end of the week I could look back with a modest degree of satisfaction.

Everything I cooked had been eaten, and everyone had been mildly complimentary. But it was somewhat stressful. I was never relaxed and had no confidence whatsoever. Later, at other lighthouses, I found cooking easier but continued to lack confidence.

When my week as cook was over it was time to go ashore. My fortnight on Muckle Flugga had come and gone. We had arrived on a Sunday so we left on the Sunday but this time the weather was very different. There was not breath of wind and the sea was lying like a mirror, a ladies' landing. Lowry took the *Grace Darling* alongside the Comb and ropes were hardly necessary. The lightkeepers coming on to the rock could step ashore and Hugh Arthur and I could step aboard. This time there was no need for any shouting or histrionics from Lowry and the relief was completed smoothly and gently.

When we arrived at the shore station at Burrafirth Hugh invited me to his house to meet his wife, Anne, and their family. I phoned for a taxi to take me to the ferry at Belmont and Anne made tea while we waited.

CHAPTER 9

BACK TO SUMBURGH

A FEW days before I left Muckle Flugga a message came through from Mr Dickson telling me to return to Sumburgh Head until further notice. I understood by this that I might soon be on the move again but this was all part of the life of a supernumerary.

On the way back to Sumburgh I was allowed to stay at home, with my parents, overnight. This concession may have been granted in any case but being Sunday there was no ready-made way of getting to Sumburgh that day. When I arrived the next day I found that little had changed. No new lightkeeper had come to replace Robbie Sinclair and Andy Flaws had been covering the period that I had been away. I moved back into the empty house and soon settled down to the routine of the station. Now I felt I had some experience behind me and was at ease with the watchkeeping.

Lightkeepers' houses were only partially furnished so my accommodation was somewhat Spartan, but I had the place to myself. I was comfortable and happy. For the first time since I became a lightkeeper I had a social life again. I had a day off each week the same as anyone else and I was able to go to Lerwick for a day out.

On one such trip I met, to my great surprise, Frank and Willie. They had finished at Muckle Flugga and were on their way to another lighthouse. We had a dram and something to eat together. It was good to see them again. I did not realise it at the time but in the years to come Willie Manson was to become a really good friend.

By this time Margaret's holiday at home was finished and she had gone to London to work on the fourteenth floor of the Shell Centre in a dining area that fed many hundreds. It was all part of her college course. I felt sad that we missed out. We had both been in Shetland at the same time but had scarcely seen each other. It was back to writing love letters and as many phone calls as we could fit in. At this same time a young man from Cullivoe, my home area, was also working in the Ness. He was David MacFarlane, a student at agricultural college but spending the summer at the Quendale Farm gaining outside experience. He was in Quendale for much the same reasons as Margaret was in London. After we made initial contact we arranged to meet for a pint, or four, in the Sumburgh Hotel. Neither of us had transport so I had to walk down from the lighthouse and David had to walk all the way from Quendale. One thing that was clear was that by the time I toiled all the way back up the hill to the lighthouse the effects of any alcohol were well worn away.

One night, in the hotel, a stranger came and spoke to me. He turned out to be Willie Young from Scatness. I knew of him. We were connected very loosely through marriage. He invited me to visit him and his wife, Anna, who originally came from Haroldswick. It was now nearing the end of the summer and before I bade them goodbye Willie took a spade and dug up a small bucketful of potatoes. The Ness is famous for the quality of its potatoes but this must have been the best of the best.

An unexpected perk came my way when I was offered a trip in a helicopter. Helicopter pilots, based at Sumburgh Airport, visited the lighthouse quite often. One of them said he had two spare seats in the aircraft he was flying out to the oil rig Stayflo, 110 miles east south-east of Sumburgh Head. I did not need to be asked twice but I had to get Eddie's permission. Not only that, but there were three lightkeepers and as junior man I was least likely to go. Eddie was entirely democratic in his approach. He said we would draw lots. As it happened he was the one who lost out, so Jimmy Watt and I made the trip. At the airport we had to sign a disclaimer, an agreement that in the event of any accident we had taken the trip entirely at our own risk.

The weather, on the day, was disappointing; heavy drizzle and poor visibility. The cabin of the helicopter had been stripped of everything non-essential. It was cold and incredibly noisy. In the event we saw nothing. We lifted off and within seconds the ground had disappeared in the gloom and the next thing we saw was the Stayflo. When we landed we were told to keep our seats. We could not we allowed out of the aircraft for security reasons. We may have been industrial spies! In about five minutes we were airborne again and on the way back to Sumburgh. The weather never improved so an adventure that I had looked forward to turned out to be a damp squib. Nonetheless, it was my very first time in a helicopter and it was to be some time before helicopters were used regularly in the lighthouse service.

Another event I was able to attend was the Johnsmas Foy in Lerwick Town Hall. Johnsmas was the feast day of St John and a day that for fishermen was second only to Jül in importance.

Each year Dr Tom Anderson organised a concert even if it was a bit later than the actual day. What was important to me was that the Cullivoe Fiddlers were among the performers and predominant among them were Margaret's father, Willie Barclay Henderson and her brothers Angus and John. It was a brilliant night, a superb example of Shetland's rich and varied musical talent.

The following day, a Sunday, they came down to Sumburgh and I was proud to show them where I was working and the kind of work I did. After they left it was a case of settling down to the routine of watchkeeping.

The most important thing that happened during my two spells at Sumburgh Head, other than Margaret's visit, was that I got my first pay packets. At that time supernumeraries were paid in cash. The money arrived in a medium-size biscuit-coloured registered envelope. My hands shook with excitement as I opened the first one. Remember, I had been unemployed for many months and had no money even when I was working. In the envelope was £90. This might not sound very impressive for a month's wages but to me it was a fortune and I could look forward to similar pay every month. I blessed the day that I had the wit to join the lighthouse service.

All good things come to an end, as the saying goes. The time had come for me to leave Sumburgh Head and move on. I was reminded of Superintendent Smith's warning that I would not always be at Sumburgh. The instruction from Mr Dickson was that I was to proceed to Fair Isle North the following day.

CHAPTER 10

FAIR ISLE

THE summer night was dark and dawn broke grudgingly revealing angry grey seas. The wind was force eight from the south-east and Eddie thought it unlikely that the ferry, the *Good Shepherd,* would attempt the crossing. Nonetheless, she appeared off the Head at 11am, bobbing up and down in the water like a cork.

The landing place for the Fair Isle boat is at Grutness, a little harbour that lies in the shelter of Sumburgh Head. As soon as it tied up at the pier Eddie took me, complete with belongings, to the *Good Shepherd*. The crew could tell us what we knew already, that it had been a very rough trip.

The return journey to Fair Isle was in some doubt but a decision would be made at one o'clock, by which time the tide would have turned. When we returned at the appointed time the skipper, James Stout, said we were going to sail. The weather was no worse and the shipping forecast promised some improvement. This was not the most welcome news for me. I am an indifferent sailor and did not look forward to this trip.

Every recent ferry serving Fair Isle has been called *Good Shepherd*. This one could carry twelve passengers and the seats in the cabin had started life in a coach. They were fixed solidly to the deck. I knew that my best chance of staving off seasickness was to wedge myself firmly in a seat and move with the boat. I raised my knees and braced them against the seat in front and awaited the ordeal to come.

"Is do wantin a bag tae spew in?"

This was the rather ominous question asked of me by Alex Stout. Every seat was taken and Alex went around giving out bags. No sooner had we left the pier than the pitching and rolling started. Faces around me quickly altered to various unhealthy shades of pastel and bilious green. My own hue would hardly bear close scrutiny but I was never actually sick. Many of the others were and Alex had to come and collect full bags. He was like a waiter in reverse, throwing full bags overboard and giving new, empty bags to the suffering.

The water between the Shetland mainland and Fair Isle is known as the Sumburgh roost. The roost is a notorious stretch of water. Even with fine weather and in the big ferries that run to Aberdeen you can never cross the roost without being aware of it. This crossing took four and a half hours and it seemed an age. It still ranks as one of the worst boat trips I ever made.

At last we came into North Haven, the landing place in Fair Isle. The relief at returning to dry land was stupendous and I was met by my new workmates from the North light, Kenny Clarke and Robert Corbett. Kenny was one of the few Englishmen employed by the NLB. He was unmarried and his mother lived with him at the lighthouse. Robert, like myself, was a supernumerary, somewhat senior to me. He came from Edinburgh and his previous work had been as a zookeeper. He retained a great interest in animals and wrote articles for the *Northern Lighthouse Board Journal* about them. For the next five weeks Robert and I were to share an empty house at the station.

It was a little unusual to have two supernumeraries at one station but as it happened two assistant keepers had departed at the same time. As I was to discover, Fair Isle North was not the most popular station. Not only was Fair Isle remote from the rest of Shetland but the north light was remote from the rest of Fair Isle. The island is only three miles long but, at the north light, lightkeepers and their families had no neighbours. This was the one downside to my time on the isle. I never had the opportunity to meet and get to know the people. All the folk live near the south end and the south light was far more a part of the community. The north lighthouse station had a Land Rover for staff to use. Fair Isle North was not classed as a schooling station. It was considered too difficult, in the absence of public transport, to get children to and from the island's primary school. The Land Rover enabled the lightkeepers to go to the shop and anywhere else they needed to go.

Because Fair Isle had a small population, around the seventy mark, it was hard to sustain a profitable shop. Prices tended to be dearer than on the Shetland mainland but there was an unwritten law that everyone bought from the local shop. In the case of lightkeepers, they kept receipts from the shop and the lighthouse board paid whatever percentage of the total was deemed to be freight charges.

The islanders took a lasting pride in their home. The sense of community was strong and the average age surprisingly low. Much had been done to improve the quality of life on the island. For example, they had a network of generators that provided electricity. They made the most of their unrivalled reputation for making the fine patterned knitwear which is world famous. In

Fair Isle North lighthouse. © *Dave Wheeler*

the migratory seasons there no better place to see rare birds. The National Trust owns Fair Isle, and without doubt this has brought benefits, but the islanders have played a full part. Newcomers were welcome and whenever a house or croft became vacant an applicant from outwith the isle was favoured. This has played no small part in keeping the population stable. The only negativity I ever encountered was that some folk seemed slightly defensive. They assumed, wrongly, that someone like me was in Fair Isle against my will.

To return to the lighthouse station, it was not too hard to see why it was not popular in the service. The lightkeepers' houses were all in a block and the assistants lived in first floor flats. The heating came from coal fires and the cooking fuel was bottled gas. Electricity was very limited. A generator was started every day at dusk.

It was clear that the plumbing and wiring had been added long after the houses were built. The walls were covered in pipes and bulges that made any kind of decorating a nightmare. Nonetheless, Bob and I were comfortable and contented in the house we shared. Bob was very keen on cooking so we had some great feeds. A favourite recipe of his was stuffed cabbage and stuffed onions. Onions were hollowed out, the centres mixed with minced beef and put back into the outer skin. What was left over was wrapped in cabbage leaves and the whole lot was stewed and served with gravy and potatoes.

The local shop had almost everything we needed but butcher meat had to be ordered from the mainland. I thought I would try my hand at cooking so I sent for some cheap cuts of lamb necks and shoulder. I made it into the classic Shetland

Fair Isle north lighthouse. © Dave Wheeler ➤

dish of tattie soup. Bob would not eat his without first taking photos. It was the first time, he said, he had seen soup that could be piled up.

Kenny Clarke was a good and easy principal keeper to work with and Mrs Clarke invited Bob and I in each morning for our elevenses, coffee and biscuits. Nearly all the painting and other summer work, on works orders, was finished but there was still grass to cut and a fence to put up.

Shortly before I arrived one of the keepers had had a narrow escape. He was driving the Land Rover when he went off the road and had come within a whisker of rolling over the cliff. The superintendent ordered this stretch of road to be fenced in an effort to prevent the same, or worse, happening again.

The three of us worked at this every day that the weather was good, but on the very first day, when I was the one wielding the heavy maul I missed the fencing post and broke the hammer handle. There were no spares at the station and the shop did not stock handles either. As a makeshift we used roller blind centres. At every lighthouse the lantern was covered during the daytime to prevent the sun shining through the powerful lens and the real possibility of causing a fire. The blinds were rolled on wooden poles that were the same diameter as the hammer handle. But there the similarity ended. Hammer handles are made from hickory and were tough and durable, while the wood for roller blinds was white and soft and totally unsuitable for hammer handles. But they were all we had and Kenny frequently warned Bob and I to be careful and not hit the posts too hard. Even so, the improvised handles broke with alarming regularity and had to be changed every other

Fair Isle north lighthouse and fog horn. © *Dave Wheeler*

post. Luckily there was a plentiful supply at the station but Kenny had to set aside a reserve in case they were needed for their intended purpose. I had broken the original handle and it fell to me to break the last one. We finished the fence using a stone for a hammer.

The light at Fair Isle North shows a character of two white flashes every thirty seconds. The tower is low and squat, only fourteen metres high, and the lens revolves very slowly. The clockwork was powered by a very heavy weight. Any lighter weight and the machine may well have stopped. Being so heavy made for a hard wind with two hands needed on the handle. The machine was massive and, in fact, was a machine within a machine. The auxiliary clockwork was intended to keep the lens moving while the main clockwork was being wound. The whole thing was quite complicated and lightkeepers simplified the process by giving the lens a push every time they stopped for a rest during the wind.

I found the engine room the same as the one at Sumburgh Head so there was nothing new to learn there, but anyone on watch had to be vigilant because fog was a problem here too. The foghorn was quite a distance from the dwelling houses and therefore the siren was rather less intrusive.

I was sorry when the order came for Bob to "proceed" to another station. We had made friends and as it happened I never met him again. Some time later I was disappointed to hear that he had had to leave the service because of health problems.

All this time, while Margaret was working in London, she phoned me as often as she could. I could not phone her because

Fair Isle north lighthouse. © *Dave Wheeler*

she did not have access to a phone at her accommodation. She a hard time persuading some of the telephone operators in London that there really was a telephone number Fair Isle 2.

My turn to leave Fair Isle came soon after. New assistants had been assigned to the station and to my amazement I was told to go home on leave. I had been a supernumerary for only five months and thought that leave was something that trainees like me got once a year – maybe. It was only a week and I was told to phone HQ every day in case I was needed somewhere in a hurry. To get a week off was brilliant but what made me think all my Christmases had come at once was that Margaret also had a week off before she went back to college in Aberdeen.

I said my goodbyes to the kindly Mrs Clarke and Kenny took me down to the *Good Shepherd*. By this time I had acquired some uniform so, for the first time, I travelled in a blue suit with brass buttons and a white cheese-cutter hat. I had been on the two-to-six watch so I was short on sleep but I was given a bunk on the *Good Shepherd* and was able to relax and doze on the way back to the mainland. In any case the trip back was relatively smooth; there was none of the pitching, rolling and wholesale spewing of the previous voyage.

Making generous use of the receipt book and the authority I had to spend money on behalf of the NLB, I arrived home by taxis and the ferry just after lunchtime. Of course my priority was to go and see Margaret. This I did, and there was a dinner dance in the Cullivoe hall that night so we went there. We really enjoyed our week together but it went by in a blur. It's amazing how fast time goes when you don't want it to. I dutifully phoned Mr Dickson each day and, on the Tuesday, he told me to proceed to Edinburgh on Saturday and join the lighthouse ship *Pharos* on the Sunday night.

CHAPTER 11

THE BELL ROCK

MY NEXT lighthouse was to be the Bell Rock. I suppose I had become a bit complacent. I had spent all summer in Shetland and the thought of travelling to a pillar rock via Granton came as a wake-up call. I booked a flight to Aberdeen and took the train to Waverley Station in Edinburgh.

I was booked in at the YMCA hostel. It was basic but comfortable and friendly and I had all day Sunday to rest and lounge around. I went out for lunch and had delicious fried chicken and chips washed down with a glass of beer. In the late afternoon I took a taxi and found the *Pharos* tied up at the quay.

The *Pharos* was the flagship in the NLB's fleet. She was a beautiful ship, beautifully kept with varnished wood and gleaming brass. Other ships in the fleet were the *Hesperus*, also in Granton, the *Fingal*, stationed in Oban and the *Pole Star* in Stromness.

When I boarded the *Pharos* I was shown to the mess room and introduced to the master, Captain Neil MacFarlane. He lost no time in handing me a mug of tea and asking a great many questions. I was astonished at his depth of knowledge about Shetland. He seemed to know everyone that I knew.

Capt MacFarlane was from the island of Coll and was, in fact, the ship's first officer. He was acting master because the regular master was on holiday. Neil MacFarlane, I came to know, had made a great reputation for himself as a second mate. On those ships it is the second mate who is in charge of making the actual reliefs at lighthouses; they were the coxswains of the launches that took the lightkeepers from the ship to the rock station. They were a breed of daring, swashbuckling seamen who had skill, style, cool judgment and the ability to react instantly to any sudden change in the sea and landing conditions. It seems that, before his promotion, Neil MacFarlane was foremost amongst them.

The time spent in his company was pleasant and later I was given a bunk in a snug cabin where I had a good night's sleep. The following morning, after breakfast, other lightkeepers joined the ship. As well as the Bell Rock the *Pharos* carried out reliefs at the Bass Rock and the North Carr lightship. I knew none of them but gradually learned who was going where and that a middle-aged man with a thin face and a pointed head was an assistant lightkeeper at the Bell Rock and therefore my travelling companion. I shall call him Norman Wilson. At first glance he radiated neither charisma nor charm. As it turned out my first impressions were accurate if a little generous to the man.

Because of the tide times the Bell Rock was to be the last relief of the day. The first was the Bass Rock, where one keeper was landed and another picked up. Next was the North Carr Lightship. Here four men were landed, one of them a very friendly Orkney man called Lowry Craigie. He told me he was leaving the service and going to set up his own business in Kirkwall dealing in clocks and the repair of clocks and watches.

Looking at the lightship I pitied anyone who had to endure a whole month on it. The lightship was anchored, of course, and lying broadside on to the steep swell, rolling like a tub. It was a motion that would have turned me up in no time. It appeared to be a most unfriendly environment. It was in fact Scotland's only lightship.

In difficult conditions the relief was made and we continued on to the Bell Rock. Even getting into the small boat presented something of a challenge. The boat would career up and down the ship's side, rising and falling seven or eight feet. One at a time, but me first because I was the junior man, we had to climb down a rope ladder hung over the ship's side. It was extremely dangerous to go too far down because you could get your legs crushed between the rising boat and the ship's hull. If you did not go far enough you had to risk jumping down into the boat and not only was there a danger of twisting ankles or breaking bones but you could land on top of someone, causing them injury.

I got safely in, albeit without much dignity, and so did Norman Wilson. The boat was cast off from the *Pharos* with Second Mate Swanson at the helm. It was a bitterly cold October day with a force six wind, heavy drizzle and a nasty swell. When we got close to the lighthouse it was clear that we were too early. The landing at the Bell Rock is tidal. At low water there is so much rock exposed that a boat can get nowhere near the lighthouse and at high water the landing stage is under about eighteen feet of water and lightkeepers cannot leave the safety of the tower, so the tide has to be at exactly the right state. This gives a short window of opportunity to complete the relief. In the end we had to circle for more than an hour before the ebb tide was far enough back.

I had no oilskins of my own but the mate on the *Pharos* had given a loan of a suit. I was grateful because the rain and the salt spray would have soaked me to the skin. As it was I was chilled to the marrow and really glad when finally coxswain Swanson shouted out to all that he was going in. The landing was a narrow iron grating bolted to the rock and again, as protocol demanded, I was first out of the boat.

As soon as the men were transferred the cargo was unloaded. It had not escaped my notice that there seemed a lot of it. As I later discovered it was annual stores and it was my bad luck to arrive at the same time. The boat lost no time setting off back to the ship and we took in the ropes and carried the stores to the base of the lighthouse.

Once inside I was told to climb the ladder to the first floor and there I would find a length of rope. This I was to lower down and then haul up whatever was on the end of it. I was close to where a generator was running. It was very noisy and the heat was overwhelming after the extreme cold of the boat. I did not even have time to take off the oilskins. Soon the sweat was flowing freely and I was hauling to the utmost of my strength. One item seemed almost too big for the opening but it did come through and when I had time to look I saw it was a fridge.

Later, over a cup of tea, I met the principal keeper, John McWilliam. I had never met John before but I knew of him. He had been an assistant at Muckle Flugga and was married to Eliza Henry who belonged to Sellafirth, about three miles from my home.

"Can you do the weather?" John wanted to know.

I could not. I had never been to a weather station before. Some, but by no means all, lighthouses doubled as weather observatories and reports were relayed to the Met Office every three hours. The weather reports were used in two different ways. As well as being used in the compilation of weather forecasts the observations were recorded in a big ledger and used in the study of climate and how it might change. The observations included the amount of cloud and cloud types, wind speed and direction, barometer readings, temperature and the temperature of a wet bulb so that the relative humidity could be computed. Sea temperature was taken once a day.

All this information had to be gathered and translated into a code, groups of five numbers, and transmitted by radio to RAF Leuchars in Fife. It was clear that a crash course in weather observation was vital. I found it a bit difficult to grasp all at once but was shown little sympathy. I was told, in no uncertain terms, that I had until my own watch started to learn because neither I nor the Met Office were important enough for any of the other two keepers to lose sleep over.

The weather was one thing but I also had to learn how to keep a watch and how to start the foghorn. The Bell Rock was an electric light and I needed to know how to change the massive 2.5K bulbs in the event of one fusing. I also had to know where to find things, but one way or another I got through the 10 to 2 watch.

I doubt that my weather reports made much sense. Clouds were just clouds to me at that stage. I did not know anything about stratocumulus, altostratus and cirrus, to say nothing of the dreaded cumulonimbus and the rest, like calculating dew point using a slide rule. Like everything else totally new it began to make more sense as time went on.

John McWilliam had been kind and considerate in giving me the 10 to 2 watch. It meant I could be on watch with Norman from 6 to 10 and had a chance to see what he did in a routine watch, including the weather reports. It also meant I did not have to cook any meals during my first night on the rock. At 2am I called John on watch and was free to go to bed. As principal keeper John had a room to himself. Bedrooms were very small and cramped with little room to spread out belongings. The rooms had bunk beds three high. This was necessary in the event of having artificers or workmen as extras on the rock. I shared a room with Norman. He was, of course, in bed when I turned in. I did so as quietly as possible and heard him get up and go out for his watch at 6am. I was called at 8 for breakfast and afterwards John took me to show, in detail, the station and how it worked. Norman was to be cook for the week.

It was daylight and an ebb so we went, first of all, to the top and out on to the balcony where we had an overview of the rocks the lighthouse was built on. The first thing I saw were dozens of seals lying high and dry, without fear, all around the base of the tower. I also saw many iron walkways bolted to the rock.

The Bell Rock or Inchcape Rock is a very large reef. The bigger the ebb the more rock is visible. Before the lighthouse was built it was a graveyard for ships and in an effort to protect mariners a bell was fixed in such a way that the motion of the waves rang it. That is why it was renamed the Bell Rock.

An infamous pirate known as Sir Ralph the Rover cut the bell away, hoping that his enemies and other ships would be wrecked, giving him plunder and wealth. It was a case of the best laid schemes, because Sir Ralph himself was shipwrecked on the Inchcape Rock and drowned unlamented.

When we landed on the rock I never realised that there were a number of alternate landing places. Natural gaps in the rock structure formed channels where the relief boat could approach. They were variously used depending on the weather and direction of the swell. They all had different names. Where we landed was the one most often used and was called the Fairway. Johnny Gray was another landing and there was also M'Urich and Port Hamilton.

Going down to the bottom and outside we descended the massive bronze ladder that led down on to the rocks. The entrance to the tower was about 25 feet above the base. It had to be like that to be above sea level at the highest tide. We were outside because John wanted to take a close look at a section of walkway that was in danger of detaching from the rock and would have to be cemented back into place.

Inside again John showed me the generators, two Gardner units that gave the lighthouse all the electricity it needed. The date, at the bottom of the tower, was 1809 and it was evident that it was never designed to house all that was needed in modern times so every floor was used to the full. There was no wasted space.

The lighthouse board was very aware of the danger of fire. It is to be feared in any lighthouse but in a pillar rock like this one fire is deadly. The hollow tower acts like a chimney and a colossal updraft is created. This was the case when a disastrous fire destroyed the Chicken Rock lighthouse to the south of the Isle of Man. Thankfully there was no loss of life but from that time extra precautions were taken. The Bell Rock tower had been stripped, as far as possible, of everything combustible and there was a fire alarm and sprinkler system activated by any serious overheating. It was vitally important, John explained, that nothing was stored or laid near the sensors.

There were, from top to bottom, six levels. It was a strict rule that anyone going up or down closed every hatch behind him.

No hatches were allowed to be open even for a short time. Again, this was in case of fire. At the very top there was a rope with knots in it about 12 inches apart. This was a safety rope that could be slung over the outside of the tower for men to slide down in an emergency.

The kitchen, where the lightkeepers spent most of their time, was only 11 feet in diameter. You could go up or down but any lateral movement was limited. On every floor the walls were covered in a bewildering mass of wiring and plumbing. Pipes were colour coded. Pipes carrying diesel oil were painted brown, fresh water was white, salt water blue, paraffin red and waste pipes black. All in all, the Bell Rock was the most complex lighthouse I ever worked in.

The tower is 36 metres high and the light shows a character of three white flashes every 30 seconds. The whole structure is a magnificent feat of engineering. It was the work that made the career of Robert Stevenson and began the dynasty that lasted until the 1930s. We can only marvel at the determination and stamina of the men who built the Bell Rock lighthouse in such an unfriendly and difficult place. After a level area was identified a circle some fifty feet across had to be hewn out of solid rock some eighteen inches deep so that the first layer of granite slabs could be embedded. The granite slabs were cut and shaped on the shore at Arbroath and fitted together with a precision that is well nigh unbelievable. They are, for all the world, like a wooden jigsaw puzzle.

The length of the working day was short because of the tidal nature of the site and Robert Stevenson made a bold decision. He approached the Church of Scotland and sought their

Bell Rock lighthouse. © Peter J. Clarke ➤

blessing for Sunday working. Hitherto the Sabbath was sacred and no working was allowed. The Church's senior clergy, after considering the urgency of the work and the need for a lighthouse, gave their consent, thus giving a boost to the timetable. Of course the Stevensons built many more lighthouses but the Bell Rock was, and is, an achievement that made the Stevenson family name immortal.

On my first night on the Bell Rock I was shown, as you would expect, where the toilet was. It was right at the bottom, again, as you might expect. It was a tiny cubicle with a toilet seat about the size of a primus stove but it had a lever on the right side like a hand brake. This was the flushing system; seawater was pumped through to clean it out. So small was the cubicle that no average-sized person could turn in it. The trick for anyone doing a number two job was to take their trousers down outside and back in, rather like an inelegant lobster entering a fisherman's creel. Once seated, the one bonus was that the smell of the sea masked any less pleasant stink.

In explaining this delicate procedure, John spoke from the corner of his mouth in a somewhat furtive manner. He told me that all this could be short-circuited and that, in fact, lightkeepers seldom went to the toilet. To do a pee, a "single fish", lightkeepers went on to the balcony and let rip through the cast iron railing. This sounds simple enough and so it was in calm weather but, bear in mind, the balcony was a hundred feet above sea level and a wise man took note of the wind strength and direction. A blowback was always possible.

A number two job, a "Tom Kite", was a good deal more difficult. If the toilet at the bottom of the tower was to be used the event had to be planned well in advance. If the need was urgent and delivery imminent, crisis point came long before you reached the cludgie. All those flights of stairs and opening and closing six hatches took too long for anyone cut short, so keepers had to box clever. John had the air of a man divulging a state secret when he told me the next bit. Again the balcony was the place. You spread out an old newspaper, squatted down and did the deed on the paper. When finished you wrapped the whole lot into an unlovely parcel and threw it over the side. Here again some preplanning and care was necessary. The paper might blow away and you were left with a mess to clean up and of course it might be a gale and raining, tempting some to do their "Tom Kite" in the lightroom. This was more or less acceptable but the floor of the lightroom was a grating and anyone below would have a worm's eye view of an unwelcome variety.

One really bad night, I was told, the occasional keeper spread out his newspaper on the floor of the lightroom directly above the radiotelephone. The problem was that the principal keeper was speaking to his wife at the time. He was neither amused nor comfortable, and he was like a tedered animal straining at the extreme end of the flex that connected the handset. What he said afterwards to the keeper is, mercifully, not recorded.

On the Bell Rock the need to conserve drinking water was important. There were limited storage tanks and obtaining supplies from the shore was entirely weather dependent. As well as the water, diesel oil had to taken on to the rock. There was a strange-looking contraption in the tower; I had to ask what it was and it turned out to be a plant for turning seawater into fresh water. Apparently it worked well but a serious snag became evident when it was discovered that it took more than a gallon of diesel to produce one gallon of water.

My fortnight on the Bell might have been pleasant but for the first time in my short career as a lightkeeper I had difficulty in getting on with a workmate. Norman Wilson was the problem. John McWilliam was a good boss and someone I could talk to and enjoy the company of. We had many mutual acquaintances and in the kitchen, over endless cups of tea, the conversion flowed. But Norman seemed to regard me as the lowest form of ebb life. Nothing I did was right. I never looked forward to cooking but initially I took heart when I saw the dinners that Norman produced. They were all right but were entirely plain and straightforward and it was not beyond me to produce meals of the same quality. In some respects Norman's food was pretty ordinary. The potatoes we had were Scottish and poor quality but by the time Norman dished them up, mashed, they ran between the toes of a fork. Nonetheless Norman regarded himself as a wonderful cook and expected lavish compliments and moans of appreciation after every bite. When I cooked anything, even toast at breakfast, he would hold it arm's length and his comment never varied.

"Well, you made a right bloody mess of this!"

One day, when it was my turn to make dinner, I made Scotch broth and, if I say so myself, it was good and tasty. John was quick to spike Norman's guns. He remarked on the soup and how much he was enjoying it. Norman supped in grim silence.

In the middle of the afternoon he came storming into the kitchen, shoved me out of the way, and went to the medicine chest. John asked if he was OK.

"No", he snarled. "I have a sore stomach. Must be that bloody soup."

Actually that made me feel a lot better because now I knew for certain he was being totally unreasonable.

Norman had a powerful chip on his shoulder. He was ex-Royal Navy and this, it seemed, gave him, for whatever reason, a superiority complex, and he looked on everyone else as inferior. Also, he was caught in a logjam in terms of promotion. The automation of lighthouses was in full swing so whenever one was de-manned places had to be found for the existing men, holding up the promotion of assistant keepers to principals and the appointment of supernumeraries like myself. Norman had been in the service long enough that in the normal course of events he would have been a principal keeper.

Trainees had to bear the brunt of these grievances and as I found out later I was not the only one with cause to dislike Norman Wilson. In the bedroom I was not allowed to leave anything, especially clothes, lying around, but the same rule did not apply to Norman. One night when he left the window open, I ignored the bird that came in and allowed it to make a mess of the uniform Norman had left out of the wardrobe.

It was an unwritten rule that in the afternoons the man on duty was given the kitchen to himself. It was the only time during daylight hours that a lightkeeper had any privacy. It was the opportunity to have a wash. In a pillar rock lighthouse there is no shower or bath. Men had to make do with a sponge down from a basin of warm water on the floor. This simple pleasure, too, was denied me. Norman never left me alone in the kitchen. He was always there as if he was daring me to complain about his presence.

In the evenings the rule was that each man, night about, decided what was watched on TV. If John was in bed Norman always overruled my choice. If I really wanted to watch something in particular I had to declare my preference for another channel. There were three channels, so this gave me a 50-50 chance of seeing what I wanted to see. When John was there I did have a say but Norman never stopped grumbling. When I had had my interview in HQ it had been drummed into me that no workmate in the lighthouse service was forever. Workmates came and went and I only had to endure Norman Wilson for two weeks.

One nasty moment had nothing to do with him. The cook was expected, among many other jobs, to wind up the clock which hung high up on the kitchen wall. What the rooms in the lighthouse lacked in floor space they made up for in height. To reach the clock I had to stand on tiptoe on a chair. As well as the need for winding, on this occasion it needed to be set to the correct time. It was a minute or two slow and a single knurled knob did both jobs. To wind it up the knob had to be turned clockwise but to set the time the knob had to be pushed in. This I did at the extreme length of my reach. I was aware of the clock sliding up the wall but to my horror it unshipped itself from the hook and shot up into the air. It never went high enough to touch the ceiling but went through a graceful arc and was going to drop and get smashed on the floor well behind me. In a contortion that came from miraculous desperation I arched my back and caught it, jumping backwards and down to the floor. Thinking about this and looking back it almost makes my eyes water and I know I could never do it again, not in a million years. The clock was none the worse and I never found it necessary to tell Norman about it. Talk about getting off the hook!

I assumed I was to be on the Bell Rock for two weeks only but I had never been told for sure. Midway through the second week the confirmation came. I was told to report to the office before proceeding to Rubh Ré.

The relief was uneventful. John and I left the rock leaving Norman for the second fortnight of his tour of duty. This time the ship was not the *Pharos* but the *Hesperus*. Both vessels were stationed in Granton and each ship carried out the reliefs at the east coast lighthouses.

On board I met a man from my own island, Willie Stewart from North-a-Voe. He introduced me to some of his shipmates. I found that many of them were former whalers and knew many Shetlanders. It was a pleasant trip ashore but I stayed on board the *Hesperus* and, after breakfast, made my way to North Bridge to see Mr Dickson.

Chapter 12

Rubh Ré

MR DICKSON'S greeting was friendly. He asked me how I was getting on and whether I was enjoying the job. He brought me up to date with expenses and told me how to get to Rubh Ré. I was as grateful for the latter as the former because I have to confess I had no idea where Rubh Ré was. It is in Wester Ross and my route there was by train to Inverness, another train to Achnasheen, and then by bus to Gairloch where I would be met by one of the lightkeepers.

When I boarded the train at Waverley Station I found myself in a compartment with an elderly lady with a rather formidable aspect. She was somewhat domineering. She vetoed smoking despite the fact that we were in a smoking compartment. She soon introduced herself as Miss Wendy Wood, one of the founders of the Scottish National Party, and I believe that she was none too pleased that I had not recognised her. Although I knew her name I had never seen her before. She was famous – or notorious – as an extreme nationalist and was mighty proud of the numerous prisons she had been in because of her "fight for Scotland and freedom". My lack of enthusiasm for her politics did little to endear me to her but she made a very interesting travelling companion.

After a short wait at Inverness I boarded the famous train to Kyle of Lochalsh and travelled at a suitably sedate pace through the beautiful Western Highlands. The train was packed, with every seat taken and I became aware, for the first time, of the benefits of wearing a uniform. Several people offered me a seat as if I had been an old lady. It was rather embarrassing but folk were friendly and willing to talk to me. A lightkeeper's uniform was quite eye-catching. It was nautical in style, with navy trousers and a double-breasted jacket with brass buttons. The hat had a brass-coloured badge and white top. The cap badge carried the motto of the lighthouse service: *In Salutim Omnium*. It is Latin, of course, and means "for the safety of all".

Many a time at lighthouses where the principal anticipated a move it was common to hear the phrase "it'll do my time", meaning he would be gone before a particular job needed doing again. One young supernumerary who had recently been issued with his first uniform was at a station where the annual inspection was taking place. The superintendent asked him if he knew what the motto, on his brand new cap, meant. "It'll do my time," was the prompt reply.

I left the train at the small village of Achnasheen and continued my journey by bus. The bus carried passengers and mail and was timed to connect with the arrival of the train. It did not follow the most direct route to Gairloch, meandering through glens, villages and byways. Again, the scenery was spectacular. It was the world of the picture postcard and Loch Maree is rightly famous as an outstanding beauty spot. Despite the pleasures of the journey I was glad when, late in the afternoon, we arrived.

Gairloch is built around the shore and inland are the mountains of Wester Ross. I was still sixteen miles from Rubh

Ré lighthouse. I had been promised that someone from the station would be there to meet me but there was no sign of anyone. To make matters worse it began to rain. On Scotland's west coast rain does not fall in half measures. The rain in Gairloch, that day, was more on the lines of a tropical thunderstorm.

When my patience ran out I phoned Rubh Ré and found a place to shelter until the station car, a nice new Morris 1100, arrived about an hour later and the driver introduced himself. I shall call him Trevor Ramsbottom. He was short, dark and hugely fat with a belly that was neither moderate nor easy. I do not wish to be insulting but he reminded me of the cast iron bogey we used to have in primary school. It had short, rather bowed legs and was supposed to be good at burning wet peats. Nonetheless, Trevor proved to be a cheerful, kindly soul and a pleasant workmate.

Trevor enjoyed, if that is the right word, a tremendous reputation as a lady's man and I had heard about him before I arrived at Rubh Ré. Long after he left the service one of his ex-girlfriends, tearfully pregnant, asked if I could help her to locate him. Sadly I could not. I have no idea what became of him.

At the lighthouse the crew consisted of a Scotsman, an Englishman, an Irishman, an Orkney man and myself. A motley crew. The Scotsman was Charlie Reid from Rhynie in Aberdeenshire. Like myself he was a trainee. He had been recently married and to say he was looking forward to his next leave was a massive understatement. Charlie and I shared the bothy, a single room with bunk beds, a small cooker, a table, two hard chairs and little else, no TV or radio. It had a toilet attached but no shower or bath. Charlie used to lie on his bunk staring at his wife's photo and saying over and over again: "Isna she an awfie bonny quine."

He would ask me to look at the photo and, of course, I had sympathy for him, but I had a bonny quine of my own that I was far away from. Charlie was my age and we became really good friends and were together for quite a time. However, he had been at Rubh Ré for ten weeks and was convinced that Mr Dickson had completely forgotten about him.

The Englishman, Trevor, was from Hull. He was the second assistant. The Irishman was the principal. His name was Bill Frazer from Belfast. He often said he spelt his name with a 'z' because, above all, he wanted to make it clear that he was not a Scotsman. At the time he was off sick, sidelined by a car accident. He had been to Inverness to see his wife, who was in hospital there. On the way back his car had skidded on ice and left the road. He broke bones in both feet but in fact he got off lightly because he was out all night on the lonely road in sub-zero temperatures.

The Orkney man was Alan Tulloch, a tall, fair-haired, rather serious man from Kirkwall. Before becoming a lightkeeper he had been a pork butcher. Alan was the same age as Charlie and I but had been in the service a lot longer. He was, in fact, the first assistant and in charge while Bill was recuperating.

Alan's wife Babs, from the Isle of Skye, was a really attractive girl, full of fun, and would have been popular at any station. Babs and Alan were kind to us, offering us the opportunity of taking a bath and inviting us in for cups of tea.

The station was a bit stark and forbidding. It was as if no-one wanted to be there, simply putting in time until due for a shift. As lighthouses go it is quite recent, built in 1910 and, unlike the lighthouse of the 19th century, it was built at sea level. This meant it was seldom obscured by fog. Early on the policy was to build lighthouses on high headlands like Barra Head and Sumburgh Head. Those and others like them spent a lot of time invisible to mariners because of fog and low cloud.

The tower was quite high, over 80 feet, and the light was exactly the same as the one at Fair Isle North, a 55mm Stone Chance that showed a character of four white flashes every fifteen seconds. The engine room was built around the base of the tower and had the usual Kelvin engines to drive the foghorn. For some reason Rubh Ré leaned. It was hardly the Tower of Pisa – its departure from the perpendicular was so slight it could not be detected by the naked eye – but it was a problem because the massive lens, floating in its bath of mercury, did not run true. A counterweight was fitted to allow it to run accurately but mercury spills were frequent. Sometimes mercury ran all the way down the stairs and collected at the bottom. This meant the station had to keep an unusually large store of mercury. It came in containers about the same dimensions as a family-sized can of soup. It was well-nigh unbelievable that something so small could be so heavy. Each one weighed 90 pounds and to carry one to the top of the lighthouse required no small effort.

Charlie and I laid down some rules for ourselves on how we shared the bothy. One of them was that the man on watch stayed out except in the daytime when we were both awake anyway. During the night the man on watch was supposed to stay in the lightroom. To leave it was forbidden.

The light had to be wound up every hour and, like the Bell Rock, Rubh Ré was a weather station and observations had to be recorded every three hours. The only difference was that here we took the ground temperature while at the Bell ground was non-existent so sea temperature was taken instead.

Charlie and I ate together and took turns at cooking and we got on well in every respect. Our daily entertainment was to go each afternoon to visit the Frazers. Bill was about to be transferred to the Mull of Galloway so we helped him to pack his effects into his boxes ready for removal. Mrs Frazer was in poor health but regarded this shift as good news. She belonged to Drumore and the Mull of Galloway is the nearest lighthouse to it. Bill was a born storyteller and when he spoke he was in no danger whatever of being mistaken for a Scotsman. He had the broadest Ulster accent and I believe he deliberately exaggerated it for effect. We had frequent tea breaks and this was when the stories came out. During the Second World War he had spent a lot of time in the Mediterranean, a crewman on an air sea rescue launch. Their job was difficult and dangerous. Among other things they were expected to go close to Italy, an enemy shore, to try and rescue any Allied airmen who had been shot down.

One of the stories Bill told us was of the Christmas he spent in Alexandria in Egypt. In November he had been on leave and had managed to buy a bottle of whisky. Whisky was near to being unobtainable so this bottle was precious and he was going to keep it for Christmas. On Christmas Eve four American soldiers arrived at the dockside in a jeep.

"Heard tell you got whisky on board," said one of them to Bill. "Reckon we'll buy some."

Bill told politely them that he only had the one bottle and it was not for sale.

"We'll pay you good."

Again Bill told him he was not selling.

"You name your own price, buddie, and we'll pay it."

Intrigued, Bill asked how much they would pay for the whisky.

"We'll give you the jeep."

Bill was amazed.

"How is it that you are prepared to pay so much for one bottle of whisky?"

"It's this way buddie," answered the American. "We ain't got whisky but we got plentya goddam jeeps!"

In the end no bargain was struck because a jeep was no good to Bill. He could hardly take it on the boat with him.

By this time I had been in the service for six nearly months. At Rubh Ré, after I had settled in to the routine, I had time to take stock of the job I was doing. I saw my time at Sumburgh Head and Muckle Flugga as being on my own doorstep and therefore a bit phoney. Fair Isle was a little further away from home but still Shetland, but the time on the Bell Rock, thanks to Norman Wilson, had been downright unpleasant. I was, all in all, well pleased with the work I could do, or learn to do. The wages were reasonable, there was plenty of variety in the work and there was the opportunity to travel.

Every supernumerary looked forward to appointment. That meant attachment to one particular lighthouse and an end to probation and a performance assessment at the end of each month. As it was, supernumeraries had to be prepared to proceed to another lighthouse at a moment's notice to fill any gap caused by the illness or absence of any lightkeeper. To live in a bothy, as we did, had its drawbacks. There were no washing facilities and little privacy but it was demanded of us that we were always clean and smart and well turned out.

Necessity, they say, is the mother of invention and Charlie and I devised a novel way of washing the overalls we worked in. The sea around Rubh Ré was clean and as clear as crystal and the pebbles on the shore were smooth, red, Torridon granite. I took a pair of dungarees, threaded a rope through them, weighed them down and put them in a geo so that they were drawn gently to and fro along the bottom by the waves lapping on the shore It worked a treat. The trousers were as clean as if they had come from a washing machine. I do not know if the phrase "stone washed" had been coined in 1971 but it had meaning for me whenever I heard it. Of course they had to be soaked in fresh water to take the salt out of them but we were well pleased with the experiment.

In former times supernumeraries could expect appointment after six months but these were not normal times. The automation of lighthouses slowed everything down. Everyone's progress was dependent on seniority. There were no shortcuts. Charlie was senior to me by some months but had no idea where he was on the list. Four lighthouses were de-manned during 1971-72 – Fidra, Usneist, the Flannan Isles and Out Skerries – so sixteen men had to be relocated before any supernumeraries could move. Charlie and I had no way of knowing how long we would have to wait for appointment but we knew of some Supers who had already waited two years.

At Rubh Ré we did not get mail delivered. It had to be collected from the post office at Melvaig, five miles away. Melvaig was a small but scattered village where very little happened except a little crofting, and the TV relay station was to be found there. Supernumeraries, being the lowest form of lighthouse life, were not allowed to use the station car by themselves. We had to wait and go with one of the appointed lightkeepers to the post office or the shops in Gairloch. Mail was collected at least twice a week so it was no real problem.

Charlie quite often walked to the post office. He was desperately homesick and always looking for a letter from his "bonny quine". It was understandable because they had only spent one week together since their wedding. His belief that Mr Dickson had forgotten about him was reinforced when it was me that got word to move on. Not only that but I was given leave. Mr Dickson and I made an agreement that I could have slightly more leave if I was willing to spend it in Aberdeen. To pay my fares home to Shetland was very costly and he wanted, as far as possible, to avoid that. This suited me very well because Margaret was, by this time, back at college in Aberdeen.

Strictly speaking, supernumeraries were entitled to no more than two weeks in the year but this was impractical for two reasons. Firstly, if all the Supers wanted their leave at the same time that would cause trouble and secondly there were slack periods when Supers were not needed. To give us a few days off here and there always gave us something to look forward to.

CHAPTER 13

GO WEST YOUNG MAN

I HAD a great time in Aberdeen. I had a whole week off and Margaret and I were out most nights and I saw a number of old friends. I stayed with Joan, Margaret's married sister, who lived in Cults. Joan's husband Andrew was a seaman but was away at the time. Margaret normally stayed in the city near the college but she came to Cults for the time I was there.

The week flew past. I had been ordered to report, by phone, to the office on the Monday. Mr Dickson said things were still quiet so I could have another two days and then I was to proceed to Kinnairds Head, near Fraserburgh and report to the principal keeper there, Mr Tommy Leslie. In a dry, half-humorous tone of voice, Mr Dickson reminded me that there were buses that ran between Aberdeen and Fraserburgh. This was a gentle way of telling me that I had been too free in my use of taxis at the expense of the Northern Lighthouse Board.

On the Wednesday morning I was all ready to leave for Kinnairds Head when the phone rang. It was Mr Dickson, relieved that he had caught me before I left. There was a change of plan. He wanted me to go to Rona instead. One of the keepers there was off with a bad back and I was needed to take his place. So instead of the bus to Fraserburgh it was the train to Inverness.

When I was on my way to the railway station, wearing uniform as we always did while travelling, I fell into step with a stranger who asked what branch of the services I was in. He asked me if I smoked. An odd question, I thought, but I answered in the affirmative. He took a small pad from his briefcase and scribbled a note, tore off the page and handed it to me. He explained that he was the local manager of the tobacco company Messrs Robert Sinclair & Co and if I showed this note in their warehouse in Aberdeen I would be sold tobacco or cigarettes at cost price. I took him up on the offer. I brought eight tins of A1 hand-rolling tobacco that kept me going for quite a time.

Another noteworthy incident happened on the train on the way to Inverness. The train was quiet and I could not help noticing the young mother who was having a hard time trying to keep her four-year-old son quiet. After a while I realised that her embarrassment was caused by the fact that the boy was talking about me because he was fascinated by the uniform. After a time he seemed to lose interest until I began to eat an apple. This stirred him up like an egg whisk and he exclaimed in a loud, clear voice: "God's truth does the police eat apples!"

By the time I got to Inverness it was too late in the day to go to Skye. I stayed overnight in Inverness and took the train west in the morning. This time it was all the way to Kyle of Lochalsh. We stopped at Achnasheen before continuing westward. The railway station at Kyle was right beside the ferry terminal and the ferry was there waiting. The crossing took less than five minutes and the fare was five pence. Very soon I was in

Kyleakin and on the bus to Portree where Alex MacAulay met me.

Alex, I was to learn, was one of the nicest men I ever met in the service, a gentleman. He was the first assistant at Rona and was going to the rock with me the following morning. In the meantime he took me to his house and introduced me to his wife, Nancy, who made afternoon tea. Alex and Nancy both came from Islay and although I had no way of knowing it at the time I was to get to know them very well. Later I booked into a hotel for the night. It was near the pier and I was told to be there at nine o'clock in the morning.

In the hotel I went down to the bar for a pre-dinner drink. I got drawn into a game of dominos with three total strangers. They were all very friendly. They were aware, of course, that I was a lightkeeper and asked me where I had come from and many other questions besides. After a time they all said cheerio and left. When they had gone the barmaid asked me if I knew the man with the beard. She seemed astonished when I said I did not. He was Ron Chisholm, the "sick" man that I had come to replace. I never found out why he did not make himself known to me.

At 9am promptly Alex, the stores and myself all boarded the relief boat, *Janet MacKenzie,* and I was introduced to the skipper, Charles Macleod. Charles said grace and gave us a mug of tea before we left. The weather was foul with gale force winds and heavy rain. It was as if the tea was to soften us up for bad news.

"You will have to go in the hold," said Charles in a strong west coast accent. "The sea will be going over the boat until you can't stand on the deck. The wheelhouse can only hold two men."

The *Janet MacKenzie* was a former fishing boat about 35 feet long. It was a type of craft that could often be seen in the 1950s and '60s. In fact there were quite a few similar in the Shetland fishing fleet. I am, at the best of times, an indifferent sailor and to be locked in the cold, dark hold of the *Janet MacKenzie* was an ordeal. There was no way out until Charles and his crewman let us out. After we went in the hatches were laid in place, covered by a tarpaulin and the wedges hammered home. There was a heavy sea running that December day and the boat pitched and rolled in the most alarming fashion. We were right down at the keel with nothing to sit on. There was about nine inches of smelly water in the bilges and the only way to stay dry was to stand up and straddle the bilge water. This was acutely uncomfortable because the hold was so shallow that we had to remain crouched – doubled up, in fact. To make a bad job even worse the side planking was slippery and sometimes when the pitching and rolling was really bad our feet would slip and we had to try and hang on to the deck head. I was never actually seasick but it was about the worst two-and-a-half hours of my life.

When we heard the engine speed slow down and the *Janet MacKenzie* stopped rolling we knew we had reached our destination. The landing place at Rona is well sheltered, a landing that can be effected in all weathers, but there are reefs and baas that a boatman has to know. Going ashore that day was the principal lightkeeper Neil Thorburn and assistant Donald Macleod, both Skye men. The wind was still a good force eight and Charles was keen to get back to Portree so no time was wasted in making the relief.

The landing is some distance from the lighthouse. There was a railway line with a wagon that took the stores to the lighthouse. The slope was gentle but sufficient to allow the wagon to run down to the pier, but it had to be hauled back up again by a motor-driven winch. When we got to the lighthouse I met the third member of the crew. He was another islander, a cantankerous old devil called Rory Manson. He was employed as an occasional lightkeeper and, like other occasionals, was employed as and when needed. Rory had strong, bigoted and biased views on any subject that came up and his views were, without fail, different from the views of almost anyone else. Despite all that, I rather liked him and for the first time in my lighthouse career I was working with someone I outranked.

Originally Rona had been rated as an island station; a place where lightkeepers stayed with their families. It became a rock station when, in 1944, all the people left the island and it went the way of St Kilda. To scrape a living on Rona had never been an easy task. As an inhabited island it had a chequered history. At one point the population was all but wiped out by an outbreak of typhoid when the drains from the byres contaminated the well. Rona is quite a big island. It is six miles long but the only station I was ever at that I had no opportunity to explore. The weather never relented. It was high winds with either rain or snow for the entire fortnight of my stay.

The lighthouse is 40 feet high, had the usual paraffin light and showed a character of flashing white every twelve seconds. In the dead of winter one job that had to be done every day was cleaning the vaporiser, the double pipe through which the paraffin passed to turn from liquid to gas, which burned in the mantle. A Bunsen burner heated the vaporiser and it had to be cleaned too. Cleaning the vaporiser was not the most popular job. It was messy and tricky and therefore given to the junior man or the supernumerary. After the light was extinguished and allowed to cool it was removed from the lamp and taken to the workshop. There it was dismantled, the nipples unscrewed and the ends taken off. It was put in a vice and burned out by a blowlamp and all the soot scraped out by steel rods made for the purpose. When that was done it had to be put back together using a compound to seal the ends and nipples. It was then tested to make sure there were no leaks.

Every lightroom had several vaporisers and they were rotated, in winter, daily. Care and patience was needed to light one of those lamps. The vaporiser and Bunsen had to be heated with a burner. The burners were made of brass, about three inches in diameter and had double round wicks. They were filled with methylated spirits and lit with a match. The paraffin tank had to be pumped to the correct pressure and the vaporiser given time to heat thoroughly through and through. That done, the valves were opened and the mantle lit with a taper. To light it with a match was dangerous – a burned hand was the likely outcome. If any attempt was made to light the mantle before the vaporiser was properly heated the whole lot went up in flames and everything was blackened with soot. All this had to be cleaned before a further attempt to light up was made. Sometimes the vaporiser had to be changed as well so impatience did not pay.

Rona had no foghorn and was not a weather station so it was pretty straightforward in its working. Because it had previously been an island station there was plenty of room. Each man had his own bedroom. Like many other stations electricity was in short supply; the generators were hardly up to the job. The rooms were cold and inclined to dampness but the horrible weather was a big factor at that time.

I was interested to come across the name Janet MacKenzie in the lighthouse. She was a local heroine from the 19th century, a poor widow who kept a light burning in the window of her cottage to help the fishermen of Rona find their way into harbour around the rocks and skerries at the entrance. She had so little that she found it very difficult to pay for the paraffin but when the Commissioners of the Northern Lighthouse Board heard about Janet they awarded her a grant of twenty pounds and gave her as much paraffin as she needed to keep the extra light burning during the hours of darkness.

Contact with the outside world was none too easy. There was a VHF radio that could, in theory, link into the phone but it was old and unreliable. There was also an RT and we did 'speaks' three times a day to the control station, Eilean Glas on the island of Scalpay

Rona was a well-kept station and the food was good and plentiful but cooking presented a new and different challenge because Rory had no teeth. To keep him happy everything had to be boiled down into a paste. When I was cook I took a chicken out of the deep freeze with the intention of having it for Sunday dinner. I consulted Alex about cooking it. I told him I would stuff it and roast it with vegetables.

"Good idea," said Alex. "We have not had a roast chicken for ages."

Rory said nothing, but when I got up on the Sunday morning for my watch at 6am, he had cooked the chicken. When I looked in the pot it was clear that he had boiled the chicken for the entire duration of his watch. Not only that, but he had made his version of broth, pure gluggs that, when cold, had to be quarried out of the pot. To do that was to mash the chicken. I had to re-heat it and carefully pick out the pieces of the chicken. Even so you could see where every bit had come from.

When I said that Rory was a cantankerous old devil I did not exaggerate. Any news bulletin seemed to spark off an Alf Garnet type tirade regarding the issues of the day. He was not all negative. For example, he was strongly pro-Soviet Union, he supported Ian Smith in his Unilateral Declaration of Independence in Rhodesia and was very sympathetic towards Iceland in the Cod War.

Two things that found no favour with him were Princess Anne and Christmas trees. That year Princess Anne won the Sports Personality of the Year Award. He was furious. According to him she should never been allowed to win or even compete. So angry was he when he saw a Christmas tree in the kirk one year that he burst in during a rehearsal for a carol service, called the minister a 'fenian bastard' and demolished the tree. I believe he landed up in court and was fined for his pains.

As with the other stations it was soon time to move on. Mr Dickson ordered me to proceed back to Rubh Ré. Rory was going ashore as well. He had completed four weeks on the island. It is scarcely true to say that the relief day dawned. It was the shortest day of the year and so dark that daylight hardly appeared at all. Like every other day of my stay on Rona it was blowing a gale with very rough seas. For a time there was considerable doubt whether the crossing would be possible for Charles Macleod and the *Janet MacKenzie*.

At length they arrived in the sheltered harbour and soon we were on our way back to Skye. Charles warned that the conditions were so bad that he might take a lot longer than the usual two-and-a-half hours. Nonetheless, I refused to go into the hold and be battened down. I reckoned I was better off wet and cold on the deck than in that awful prison below decks. At least, I thought with a wry smile to myself, on deck I could see to be sick. I stayed in the shelter of the wheelhouse and took the precaution of tying myself to the mast with a length of rope. I survived the journey without vomiting.

Partly because of the winter darkness and partly because of the weather I could not see a great deal but the dangers to shipping were easy to see. Rona was the last of a line of islands with Raasay to the south of Rona and Skye to the south of Raasay.

When we arrived back in Portree and secured the *Janet MacKenzie* alongside the pier Charles invited me to come with him to the graveyard. After the kind of trip we had experienced I felt that the graveyard was probably the most appropriate place for me to be. Charles, however, did not anticipate my immediate demise. Instead he asked me if I had seen the appeal for information made by Andy Flaws in the latest issue of the lighthouse journal. What Andy wanted to know had to do with a Mrs Youngclause, a Shetland woman, who had died while her husband was a lightkeeper on Rona. She had been buried in the cemetery in Portree. Charles showed me the grave and asked me to tell Andy when next I saw him. The journal, published by the light board, was valued and looked forward to by keepers each month. Keepers themselves largely wrote it and it also contained details of all the transfers.

I stayed overnight in Skye. Rory and I had dinner together at a hotel. We got into no kind of trouble but had far too much to drink. It was a sad and sorry supernumerary who caught the bus in the morning to Kyleakin and the ferry to Kyle of Lochalsh. The gale had, at last, died down but it rained as only it can on the west coast. The train journey to Achnasheen was lovely, as always, but with a hangover from hell I took scant interest in the scenery. The same could be said for the bus journey to Gairloch but, on the mend, I arrived back at Rubh Ré in the late afternoon.

CHAPTER 14

CHRISTMAS DAY IN THE LIGHTHOUSE

IT WAS 23rd December and going to be my first Christmas away from home. I had worked away from home often in the past but always there had been Christmas holidays. The fact that Margaret was at home from college for the festive break did nothing to lessen my mounting homesickness.

Although I had been away from Rubh Ré for a short time I discovered big changes in personnel at the station. Trevor Ramsbottom had left and I had a new companion in the bothy. He was a small, fair-haired supernumerary called Norman McIvor. He was from Orkney originally but his parents were farmers near Stonehaven. Charlie Reid had, at long last, been reunited with his bonny quine.

More importantly there was a new principal. Bill Frazer had completed his move to the Mull of Galloway and in his place was Jack Ross. Jack was one of the best-known and most senior principal keepers in the service. He had a reputation as a strict disciplinarian who was especially severe with supernumeraries. It was, therefore, with some apprehension that I made his introduction. He was also rather intimidating physically; a very big, dark-haired man with a red face. He must have turned the scales at eighteen stones or so. He did not look that tall, or fat, just big.

In the weeks that followed I learned that Jack, although totally different from Alex MacAulay, was another gentleman of our profession. It is true that no-one took liberties with him and we all worked harder than lightkeepers usually do in winter, but the station was rather weary and there was much to do.

Jack led by example. He never asked me or Norman or anyone else to do a job that he would not do himself. Another assistant, Tom Grant from the east coast, had replaced Trevor. This left Alan Tulloch as the only member of the crew surviving from my previous spell of duty at Rubh Ré.

I quickly settled into the routine of the station again. For my first watch back I was on the 10 to 2, not what I would have chosen because after the awful hangover of the morning and travelling all day my only ambition was to go to bed and stay there as long as possible.

The following day was Christmas Eve but we assembled for work in the morning at 10am as usual. We did not do much and Jack invited Norman and I for Christmas dinner. It was a kind act. Jack understood well what it was like to be away from family and friends and to be working all through the festive season.

Jack Ross's father-in-law was staying with them for Christmas. He was Duncan Mackenzie, a grand old man of lighthouses. Jack and his wife, Betty, did everything they could to give us a nice Christmas. Although I was far from home it was a day spent very pleasantly. Jack was a big man with an appetite to match. I will long remember him wearing an outsized paper hat and eating vast quantities of turkey and mincemeat pies, sometimes all on the same forkful!

Over an after-dinner drink a storytelling session began. I sat enchanted listening to Duncan, Jack and Betty tell of lighthouse experiences, of storms, bad reliefs and tragedies. Duncan, I believe, was unique in the service in that he worked on the building of the Rubh Ré lighthouse and many years later was also the principal there. He told us about how all the folk left the island of Stroma after the pier was built. The pier was supposed to improve the island's viability but when the construction phase was completed the men, when they were paid off, left Stroma with their families to look for a better life.

Betty told of her memories, as a child, being with her father, Duncan, and her mother on Monach, that remote, lonely and empty island off the west coast of Lewis. She told of how terrified they all were when the window blew in during the worst storm any of them had ever known.

Those islands were never inhabited. The only people to live on them were lightkeepers and their families. Shipping routes went nowhere near them and it was decided that a lighthouse there was unnecessary. Monach, therefore, became the first lighthouse to be de-manned and the first lighthouse to be discontinued.

Jack told us about the worst night of his life, the terrible night when the Chicken Rock lighthouse burned down, when Jack and the other two men came within a whisker of losing their lives. Jack was newly promoted. It was his first light as principal. Even before he got there he knew that it had the name of the worst-kept station in the service. Nonetheless he was shocked at the filth and squalor he found on his arrival. There were even swarms of maggots on the underside of the mattress on his bed.

The principal keeper that Jack replaced was an infamous character. Bill Frazer had told me that the man lived like a pig and only wore clothes if it was too cold to go around in the nude. Even some junior men and supernumeraries refused to sit with him at mealtimes until he covered up his gross, ugly nakedness. Needless to say, Jack immediately set about cleaning the place up. In doing this he did a very foolish thing. He used petrol to clean off dirt from the kitchen floor, dirt that nothing else would shift. The gas from the petrol ignited and the whole place went up like a tinderbox. With a roar the fire went up through the tower like a huge chimney and the three men were trapped above the fire. They went to the top with the fire hard on their heels. A rope that was kept in the lightroom saved their lives. Jack lowered his two assistants down, one at a time, to the rocks below. Fortunately it was an ebb. Jack tied the rope to the balcony rail and slid down the rope. Being as heavy as he was he was unable to control his descent, with the result that his hands were severely burned. When he got to the bottom he had no skin at all left on the palms; they were red raw and he was suffering unbearable pain. They managed to get into the base of the tower below the fire but that was not safe either because burning debris and molten lead was falling from above. The fire had been seen and reported so the three lightkeepers were rescued by breeches-buoy when the lifeboat arrived at first light.

Jack was summonsed to appear at HQ in Edinburgh to be disciplined. He avoided outright dismissal but his punishment was harsh. He was put back twenty-five places on the seniority list. This meant that he was no longer a principal and he was told to proceed, with his effects, to Eilean Glas, where he would be the junior assistant. A lesser man would have cut and run, resigned from the service, but Jack took his demotion bravely, stuck it out and won the respect of all who served with him. In time he was promoted again and became a role model for many.

Also on that Christmas day Duncan told us more about Rona, the island I had been at so recently. It seems that Rona had a comparatively short history as an inhabited island although by 1821 it had a population of 130 and by 1901 there were 180 with eight different surnames – Nicolson, Macleod, MacSween, MacKay, MacLennan, MacKinnon, Graham and MacRae. For one reason or another Rona never moved with the times. People became discontented when they saw their friends on neighbouring islands with electricity, telephones, roads and improved medical services.

Family by family they packed up and left. The last natives of Rona were two elderly bachelors and their crippled sister. In the end they, too, had to leave and then there were only the lightkeepers. Later some scientists were there. Their work was a military secret but it was believed it had to do with nuclear submarines exercising in the deep water in the Sound of Raasay.

Chapter 15

New Year 1972

WITH Christmas out of the way New Year loomed. Norman and I began to conspire to get booze to celebrate with. Our scheming came to nothing because the nearest place that sold drink was Gairloch, sixteen miles away. To walk there was out of the question. It did not take long to figure out that our only hope to get there was with the station car. As Supers we had no access to the car so taking my courage in both hands I broached the subject to Jack. I tried to avoid telling him that our only errand to Gairloch was to get drams but he was too long in the tooth to be fooled. He said right away that he was going to Gairloch on New Year's Eve and that we could come with him but he gave us a very stern warning that if we took drink no lapse of duty, New Year or no New Year, would be tolerated and we both had to say to him that we fully understood what he was saying.

Jack had business to attend to. He dropped us off at the hotel and said he would pick us up later. We lost no time ordering a nip and a pint each and bought our carryouts in case Jack came back too soon for our liking. We downed the first drinks in record time and ordered the same again. We had secured a place at the bar, a corner where, on a busy day, you would have to push your way out. We were a long way from the door. The door opened and in came the crew of the essy cart and it was obvious that the drink they were about to have was not the first of the day. They were noisy, unsteady on their feet and the language they used was not for polite company, nor did it seem that they were all on the same wavelength. There was a brief period of comparative quiet while they got their drinks and then all hell broke loose. They began fighting.

They were so drunk that their hostilities, for most part, took the form of swinging and missing. One of them swung a haymaker and made contact, not with the one he was aiming at, but the result was pretty impressive. The man staggered backwards, his feet left the floor and he crashed down on a table that was laden with glasses both full and empty. It was like a scene from a John Wayne film with this man flat on his back, arms and legs flailing in a welter of broken glass and miscellaneous drink. Norman and I had no way out except through the middle of this melee but Norman found the whole thing uproariously funny. I tried to keep him quiet because I foresaw the definite possibility of getting mixed up in the fracas.

It was at this unfortunate moment that Jack Ross chose to make his entrance. He had a look in the door, shook his head and disappeared again. Norman remarked to me that if he had been as big and ugly as Jack Ross he would not be frightened of a few drunken dustmen.

Hogmanay and New Year came and went. Norman and I had our dram but were mindful of Jack's warning and had no mishaps and no telling off. This new year of 1972 was one that I looked forward to with great relish. Margaret and I planned to get married in the autumn. I was sure I would get appointed within the next twelve months and I enjoyed the job I was doing.

I now had all the confidence in the world that I could cut the mustard as a lightkeeper. Norman, on the other hand, became depressed and found it hard to settle down to the routine of the station after the excitement of the festive season. One day, when he was ready to talk about it, he told me that he was going to resign.

He did not see a future in the service. He had been a Super for 21 months and had been at 20 different stations with no word of appointment and no idea how long it would take. I was somewhat disheartened by what he said. He had joined the best of a year before me and according to Norman I had at least a whole year before I had any hope of advancement.

Not that he put me off, but a house for Margaret and I to share as a married couple seemed a long way off. I persuaded Norman to speak to Jack about the situation but he was very sceptical that it would make any difference. When he told Jack he was going to resign, Jack contacted HQ immediately. He put it to them that because men had to serve so long as Supers they were getting fed up, disillusioned and looking for other work. He reminded them that, in the past, appointment rarely took more than six months. He further argued that they were losing good men who were trained to a high standard.

As usual HQ were willing to listen to valid points and promised to see what could be done to keep supernumeraries in the job. They came up with a number of measures. They produced a list showing each man's seniority. Ernie MacLean was at the top, Bob Keith second, Philip MacLeod third with Norman in fifth place. I was down at number fourteen. They also agreed to make some houses available for married Supers. These were the houses in Oban, now empty because of the automation programme. This did not speed up the process nor were the houses any good to either Norman or I but it did show that even the lowliest lightkeepers were valued.

It was around this time that we heard the sad story of Tom Grant's penis. I have changed his name for reasons which will soon become obvious. Tom was at a station where a helicopter pad was being built. It was the norm for the lightkeepers to work with the contractors and he was working, along with the rest, on a works order. On the fateful day they were running concrete. Tom had a wheelbarrow full of cement to take to the site. He is a small, fit and wiry man but when he went down the slope he was unable to control the speed of the barrow and was not strong enough to hold it back. Soon he was running at full speed and crashed into a large, earth-fast boulder.

Tom went somersaulting head over heels but in contact with the barrow and the cement. When he came to rest and gathered his senses he was immediately aware of a white-hot searing pain in his groin. Like a castrated cat he crawled inside to assess the damage. He was horrified at what he saw when he lowered his trousers. Already his underwear was soaked in blood, his genitals appeared to be a devastated area, his foreskin had been brutally flayed back until it was torn and his penis was split from top to bottom. To make matters even worse his glands were swollen until there was no possibility of returning his foreskin to its normal resting place.

At a less remote station he would have been sent straight to hospital but here a doctor had to be contacted by radio. Tom spoke to the doctor and explained, as best he could, what had happened to him. He was acutely aware that everyone within range was listening to the conversation. The embarrassment was almost as bad as the hurt.

The doctor advised Tom to soak his penis in iced water to reduce the swelling and hopefully his foreskin would move again. The following day Tom was taken ashore and admitted to hospital. His penis had to be stitched back together again but modesty forbade Tom from saying how many stitches it took. Soon he was out of hospital to become the walking wounded. He did not have to go back to the lighthouse right away. He was to be off sick until the stitches were removed and besides, his shore leave was due very shortly. Soon he felt more comfortable and could move quite freely. That is, until he went to see his girlfriend. They went to the cinema and settled down in the chummie seats at the back as courting couples do. After some kissing and cuddling Tom felt a stirring in his nether regions. At first it was a pleasant, familiar feeling but it soon became seriously painful. As his poor mangled member stiffened and reached its full erect and lustful majesty he was aware of the stitches popping one by one and the blood running down his legs. He ended up back in hospital where all the stitches had to be replaced and he received a stern warning as to his future conduct.

Norman decided to stay on in the service given the improved information and in mid-January he got word that it was time for him to move on. I said goodbye and was never to see him again. I heard that he had been appointed to Holy Island off Arran and later the tragic news that he had been drowned in a boating accident. I often regretted that I had persuaded him to stay in the service.

CHAPTER 16

PADDY'S MILESTONE

MY TIME at Rubh Ré was over too. I was told to proceed to Girvan in Ayrshire en route to Ailsa Craig. Here I was to report to another principal, Angus Oliphant, who was universally unpopular. I made the now familiar journey past the beautiful Loch Maree to Achnasheen by bus and on to Inverness by train.

The train took me to Glasgow in the middle of the rush hour. After a bit of a struggle I got on a southbound train and arrived in Girvan at 9.30 in the evening dead tired and very hungry. It is never pleasant to arrive in a strange place with nowhere to stay. I had been given an address used by travelling lightkeepers but had lost the piece of paper.

I took a taxi from the station and asked the taxi driver to suggest a place that I might stay. He took me to Mrs Forrest's small hotel. I paid him off and while I walked the short distance to the door all the lights went out. It was because the miners were on strike. The year 1972 had started off badly for many people. The mining industry was, in those days, state owned and the National Union of Mineworkers and the government of Prime Minister Edward Heath were at loggerheads. Power stations were starved of coal to fire them and, therefore, the electricity output was seriously reduced, hence the regular power cuts.

When my eyes got accustomed to the dark I went into the hotel and found Mrs Forrest. She was a nice looking lady but said she could not keep me, not only because of the power cut but because she had workmen renovating the place during the winter. So I had to go out into the darkness lugging all my belongings.

I could find nowhere to stay. Everyone blamed the power cuts but some places were closed down for the winter. Nor could I get anything to eat. I saw a dimly lit café. They had no hot food but gave me a cheese sandwich. In a dejected frame of mind I went back to Mrs Forrest's place.

Although the hotel was closed the bar was open and it was warm in there. I bought a pint of beer and tried to get my mind together. I was faced with possibility of having to spend the night outdoors. Mrs Forrest came and asked me if I had found anywhere to stay. When I told her no she said that if I were not too fussy she would make a bed for me. Not only that but she had a gas cooker. She fried me two eggs along with a plate of chips and never did food taste so good. I tried to phone Angus Oliphant. His wife told me that he was out but I would find him in the pub.

I went to the pub in question but, of course, I had no way of knowing which man in the pub was Oliphant. I relied on the fact that I was wearing uniform so he was bound to know me. As it was we were sitting next to each other and for more than half an hour he ignored me before he spoke. I thought this rather strange but it was somewhat the same as my experience in Skye. In any event we had a drink together and he told me what I needed to know, that a taxi would pick me up in the morning at 8am to take me to the pier. For the first time that day I felt relaxed. I had another drink before turning in for the night.

Always a light sleeper, I was up in good time in the morning. I had a wash, a shave and went downstairs to find breakfast. Mrs Forrest had promised it for 7.30. There was not a soul in sight. After a time I heard a noise coming from the bar. I went in and found a startled cleaning lady clearing up glasses from the previous evening. She did not know I was staying in the place but told me that Mrs Forrest was never up at this time of the morning and if I wanted breakfast I should either make it myself or go and waken Mrs Forrest. Sure enough I found the woman of the house sound asleep in bed and had to shake her before I got any response.

By this time the electricity had been restored and in a remarkably short time I was tucking into a nicely cooked breakfast of bacon, sausage and eggs. The phone rang. It was a message to tell me that the relief had been cancelled for the day owing to the weather conditions. In my hurry to get Mrs Forrest out of bed I had never thought to look out and was never aware that it was, indeed, a bad morning. I ate, and enjoyed, my breakfast, went back to bed and slept until lunchtime. In the afternoon I explored the town and went to a barber's and got a haircut.

Girvan is by the sea and the main street goes over a rounded hill. It is a typical lowland Scottish town. The street is full of the shops and cafés of a holiday resort. Many of the cafés had framed scrolls of awards for fish frying, ice cream, and so on. Mindful of the fact that the electricity might be cut off again I went for an early tea. Looking among all the fish and chip restaurants I chose the one with the most impressive credentials in the naive belief that this provided some quality assurance. How wrong could I be? The chips were nothing to write home about but the fish was disgusting and inedible. It was raw, cold, tough and grey in the middle with soggy batter. I am not too fussy about food but that was as bad as I have ever been offered anywhere.

The wind died away so in the morning the relief was on. Mrs Forrest was awake and it was all systems go. The promised taxi picked me up at 8 o'clock with Angus Oliphant already on board. The relief boat was a bit like the *Janet MacKenzie* but rather more comfortable. *Ailsa Lady* had a cabin with seats. The journey to the rock was a good deal shorter than the trip from Portree to Rona, about eight miles and taking an hour. On arrival the stores were unloaded onto a bogey on rails, which was pulled to the lighthouse in the same way as the Rona railway. Angus and I walked behind the bogey and at the lighthouse I met the third member of the crew, Bob Watt.

As usual, at a new station, I spent the rest of the day looking around and making sure that I knew enough to keep a proper watch. Although no complacency could be allowed I had, by this time, been at enough lighthouses so that I could settle in quite easily.

From a distance Ailsa Craig looks like a giant bun, rounded and domed. However when you get close you find that it is more like a bowler hat with a fringe of beach and low ground around the edges. Anyone could be forgiven for thinking that with an island 1200 feet high the lighthouse would be on the top of it. In fact the tower is a low one, 34 feet, and built almost at sea level. The bulk of the Craig towers above this diminutive lighthouse. Every lighthouse is different in detail but Ailsa Craig was built on familiar lines. From the point of view of the keepers the height of the tower is quite important. The light here had a character of flashing six white every thirty seconds. Because of the low tower the clockwork mechanism had to be rewound every twenty minutes. At other lighthouses the winding up routine was different depending on the speed of the lens which gives the light its character. At a tall lighthouse the wind lasts longer but the climb to the top is harder. If a lens revolves slowly the weight has to be heavier to avoid any danger of it stopping. On the other hand, if the lens turned quickly the weight could be much lighter and therefore easier to wind.

Although the massive lens often floated in a bath of mercury it still had to have stabilisers, steel rollers on a steel rim. These had to be oiled but oil was sparingly used, too much was counter-productive because it formed a bow wave in front of the roller. The oil came from sperm whales because it was the only oil known, at that time, where the viscosity was unaffected by temperature.

Ailsa Craig was the only lighthouse I was at that had twin foghorns. Each horn was a long way from the compressors and there could be problems in maintaining a sufficient supply of air to the sirens. The engines that drove the compressors were three cylinder 66hp Kelvins as opposed to the usual twin 44hp engines. The size and power of the engines made no difference to the way they were operated but the fact that the horns themselves were so far away meant they were less intrusive and less noisy.

To my surprise Bob Watt turned out to be a Shetland man from Lerwick. He had close Scottish connections; his folks came from the Moray Firth area. Bob has a strong fishing background and his uncle was the late Ronnie Aitken, a highly respected fisherman who used to live in my island, Yell. I knew Ronnie very well. In fact he befriended me when I was a boy. He was, at that time, skipper of a small seine net fishing boat called the *Village Maid*. I had a great ambition to be a fisherman and Ronnie went well out of his way to help me. However, I failed as a fisherman because I never conquered seasickness. He gave me the benefit of all his knowledge and experience but the longer I was at sea the worse I got until I was so weak that I had to be helped home. One of his 'cures' which was more effective than the rest was smoking. Smoking can also make a youngster sick and by smoking at sea you could have one sickness counteract the other. Even if this logic is questionable the fact that I was allowed to openly smoke – I was thirteen at the time – was a big deal to me and for a time it did seem to work. I stuck it out for two summers but I eventually I lost heart, gave up and decided that the fishing was not for me.

Bob Watt provided me with another pleasant surprise. He was a good fiddle player. He was a pupil of renowned tutor Gideon Stove from Lerwick, the same man that taught the great Willie Hunter. Bob had his fiddle with him and one night I persuaded him to play for me. It was then, for the first time, that Principal Lightkeeper Oliphant showed his darker side. He came through with a face like thunder and put a stop to the music. He claimed he could not get to sleep. He was a man to tread canny around. Bob simply said sorry and put the fiddle away.

Two other things that rather spoiled Ailsa Craig was the fact that the whole island was alive with snakes and rats. The snakes were of the harmless grass variety but the rats were a real menace. If any door was left open they were in at once. It was not unusual to find vegetables gnawed and ruined.

Ailsa Craig has many interesting features. It is mainly made of granite and there used to be a quarry that produced curling stones. It is plain to see where the stones had been drilled and there are many discarded stones, stones that had flaws that caused them to be rejected.

At one time wild goats roamed the island but, long ago, they were hunted to extinction. Angus used to prowl around the beach wearing jackboots and carrying a rifle. He was sad about the loss of the goats; he would have enjoyed shooting them. As it was, all he could do was to take a pop at the odd rabbit.

Although it was February the weather was beautiful, more like late April or May. One day I set out to climb to the top of the island. Angus gave me directions. There is a path for most of the way if you know where to find it. Soon I was on a higher level and the path spiralled part of the way around. The way up is too steep to head straight for the summit. About halfway up there is a grassy ledge and the ruins of a medieval monastery. There is very little of it left and I could only marvel at the faith and dedication of the monks who lived there. Their lives must have been hard. They must have struggled to survive, their existence Spartan and marginal. At the end of the monk's ledge there is the most difficult section of the climb. There is a fast flowing stream straight down the steep slope and the only way up is through the water.

Having passed that the going got a little easier again but the spiral changed and now went in the opposite direction. When I had walked upwards and about halfway around the island the direction changed yet again. By this time I was leg weary and sweating like a horse. I was wondering just how much further I had to go when suddenly I was there. I had reached the top. The summit is quite small but on this lovely day the view was stupendous. With the sun over my shoulder I spent a long time looking at the view. I could see the Scottish mainland, England and Ireland. I spent time too looking at all the initials scratched on the rocks.

Soon I began to feel really cold. After sweating so much the wind up there was sharp and biting and there was no shelter so I started down again and arrived back at the lighthouse in time for tea.

All in all, my stay on Ailsa Craig was a pleasant one. Like Rona it used to be an island station. Families as well as lightkeepers used to stay on it so there was no shortage of room. Food supplies were plentiful. Bob was a good cook and, if I say it myself, I acquitted myself quite well in the kitchen.

I was a fortnight at Ailsa Craig. Bob and I went ashore together on the Saturday. I had been ordered back to the Bell Rock. I retraced my journey to Glasgow and went on to Edinburgh. I was to report to the lighthouse ship *Hesperus* on the Sunday night.

I required accommodation on the Saturday night so, again, booked into the YMCA. This low cost hostel was entirely adequate for my needs. On the Sunday after breakfast I had a walk around and had a lovely dinner of roast chicken in a restaurant close to the hostel. In the late afternoon I took a taxi to Granton and boarded the *Hesperus*.

CHAPTER 17

THE BELL AGAIN

NEEDLESS to say I was curious to know who I would be on the rock with. Truth to tell I did not care that much as long as Norman Wilson was not one of them. I was kept in suspense until morning because all the lightkeepers lived in Salvesen Crescent and had no need to join the ship until morning.

When Norman Wilson's bullet head with its long miserable face appeared I was disappointed but not really surprised. His greeting was friendly enough but it was hardly reassuring. I was confident that I would survive another two weeks of his tender care but I could not entirely suppress the thought that what I was about to endure was like going to Barlinnie with a hyena for a cellmate.

Also on board the *Hesperus* was the far more welcome face of John McWilliam. He introduced me to a supernumerary who was on his way to the Bass Rock. This young man was Andy Marshall who, in a very short career in the service, had made a name for himself for all the wrong reasons. On his way to his very first lighthouse he had missed the plane and to add insult to injury had sworn at Mr Welsh, the personnel officer, when he had been given a telling off. Later he had refused to leave a station when told to do soon the grounds that he might lose the food that he had bought for his needs. Besides, he said, he had no money.

His worst ploy was yet to come. He was at a rock station. He fell down the stairs and wrecked the gas cooker in the process. He spent the next two days in bed claiming that he was in so much pain he could not get up or keep a watch, let alone do any harder work. Of course HQ had to be told and in the end they decided to bring Marshall ashore. This decision was not taken lightly. The lighthouse ship had to be diverted from its normal schedule, a replacement keeper found, picked up, and taken to the rock. Marshall was duly helped onto the ship and into bed. When they arrived back at the mainland an ambulance was waiting at the quayside to take the injured man to hospital. When the ship was secured alongside and the gangway lowered the bold Marshall got up, walked ashore, nodded to the ambulance crew and walked off up the pier as right as rain, swinging his kitbag. His back problems had, like magic, melted away. The fact that he survived this fiasco occasioned no little astonishment through the entire service. He seemed proud of his record. He seemed to think that he had, somehow, got the better of all authority. But his reign of mayhem as the Super from hell did not last long. Whether he was sacked or managed to anticipate the inevitable is uncertain but, in any event, he disappeared from the lighthouse scene in total ignominy.

On the way to the Bell Rock that day dinner was served in the mess room of the *Hesperus*. I noticed that Norman Wilson was conspicuous by his absence. John told me he was ill. He had a violent headache, was sick and in a bunk in a darkened cabin. John asked me to go and check on him and ask if he was well enough to eat any dinner. Although I made no secret of the fact that I did not like the man it was impossible not to feel sorry for him. He looked ghastly. He was very ill, unable to get up and there was no question of him eating anything. I spent most of the afternoon at his bedside attending to his needs, which included cleaning out the pans he had vomited in. It did, I am bound to admit, occur to me that maybe he would be too ill to land on the Bell and I would, after all, escape his presence on the rock.

With this in mind I went to see John McWilliam because I believed that maybe he did not realise how poorly Norman was. John had reported the matter to the captain but the thought and the hope was that Norman would have made a sufficient recovery by the time that we got to the Bell in the early evening.

John said Norman had a history of migraine, that the bad headaches only lasted a few hours and then he was all right again. Later John went to see Norman. When he came back he said that maybe we would have to help Norman into the boat and into the lighthouse.

Norman was determined to land on the rock. He did not want HQ to know he had a medical problem. He was scared of being sent for a medical or indeed any investigation of his health. I was only a lowly supernumerary but I told John that I wanted it recorded that I was unwilling to go on to the Bell Rock with a man who was so sick that he had to be carried. It is a difficult enough lighthouse for fit men. It is no place for wounded soldiers. John noted my concern and when we came near to destination he went to see Norman and the captain again. In the end it was decided to take Norman back to shore and to hospital if necessary.

I was pleased enough to see the back of Norman Wilson but his illness raised the question of who his replacement would be. I thought that perhaps one of the lightkeepers due for shore leave might stay behind but a young seaman was pressed into service as an emergency lightkeeper. He was a very pleasant lad called John Blane. He had been a supernumerary for a short time and therefore knew something of how lighthouses worked. He had been promised that another lightkeeper would replace him as soon as possible and I pessimistically expected Norman to make a triumphant comeback.

How quickly things change. On my last spell on the Bell I was the lowest form of lighthouse life, a miserable kick-around for Wilson to vent his spite and wrath on. Now, a few months later, I was the trusted first assistant, a man accredited with knowledge and experience of the complex Bell Rock. I knew where stores were stowed, how to do the weather reports unaided, where to find things and I was, in short, John McWilliam's right bower. Perhaps the most telling aspect of my enhanced status was that John could remember my name. On my first stint I was, for the first week, Robbie and for the second week I was James.

The following afternoon the ship returned and to my delight it was not Norman that replaced John Blain but another Super, Jock Torbert. Jock and John had much in common. They both came from the same county, Wigtownshire. Jock had joined the service late. He had just scraped in below the maximum age of 35.

As well as his age Jock had had a close call at his medical. His legs had been badly damaged in an accident. He was pushing a car on icy roads when another car, unable to stop, ran into the back, crushing his legs between the two bumpers. He was in hospital for many weeks and fears were expressed that he might never walk again.

Although Jock had been in the service proper about the same time as me he had been the occasional keeper at Killantringan for years before that. He proved to be a good workmate and I will always remember his slant on healthy eating. He frowned on anything fried so instead he put things like bacon and sausages into the frying pan with generous amounts of fat and put the whole lot under the grill.

The Bell Rock, second time round, was a different place altogether. I knew it well enough that I could relax. I had no worries about keeping a watch and was confident making the weather reports. Through speaking to them on the radio I got to know some of the men on the North Carr lightship. The North Carr had a double crew and was relieved in the same way as a lighthouse. A number of Orkney men worked on the lightship. One that I spoke to often was Lowry Craigie, although he was soon to leave. He still wanted to set up his watchmaker's shop in Kirkwall. The two skippers were Jock Leask and Tommy Henderson.

Like all lighthouses the Bell Rock had a library. Reading was always a popular pastime among lightkeepers. I read *Papillion*, the story of the Frenchman who was wrongly convicted but escaped from the notorious penal colony of Devil's Island off the north coast of South America. I felt close to that unfortunate man and found myself wondering if Devil's Island was much worse than the Bell Rock with Norman Wilson as a guard. During this period I experienced, for the first time, really bad weather at the Bell. The amount of movement in the tower could be quite alarming. Big waves crashed against the tower and the way it shuddered and shook made me wonder if Stevenson and his engineers were as clever as they were made out to be. With spray flying past the windows and the noise of the sea and the howls of the wind it did not feel like a safe place to be. But I told myself it had stood for 160 years and had seen many a worse night. John said they had to stop divers working on a wreck nearby. They were blasting to clear the site but the impact on the tower gave real cause for concern. Every explosion compromised the hue of the lightkeeper's underwear.

On another day when the weather was quiet again we got another serious fright. We were sitting at the table eating our dinner when there was an almighty bang. The whole place shook, dishes rattled in the cupboard and we all jumped to our feet as one. I nearly put my fork up through the roof of my mouth. It was a sonic boom. RAF Leuchars was on the Fife coast and we often saw fighter aircraft flying past. This one had broken the sound barrier and this was what gave us the scare. After what we said in the way of expletives it would be no big surprise if the pilot of that aircraft felt his ears burning.

On another stormy night I have to confess to being homesick. It was Adaline and Alex's wedding night. Adaline Jamieson was a close friend and I went to school with her husband-to-be Alex Moar. The wedding was taking place in Cullivoe, my home village, and in the very same kirk and hall as would host my marriage to Margaret later in the year.

Next day the weather was better and my homesickness had gone. Outside, every day with the ebb, dozens of seals used to lie up on the rocks. They seemed to understand that the lightkeepers would never harm them and one was so tame it would allow its belly to be scratched with a stick.

When Jock Torbet was the cook John and I did some work extra to the routine. Summer work had not started in earnest but John was keen to do some needful repairs to the Fairway landing. Winter storms had undermined some parts of the grating and it was vital that this was arrested, a stitch in time and all that. In this case some of the pillars supporting the grating had worked loose and this compromised the safety of the landing area. With the weather good and the ebb big we mixed quick drying cement and pointed in the loose metalwork. Jobs like this have to be done and from John's point of view it was good to get this out of the way.

Inside the tower John gave me the job of painting pipes. On the face of it this sounds a simple task but, remember, the pipes were all colour coded and close together. Not only that, but they had to be traced and followed up and down six floors. Woe betide the man who painted a pipe the wrong colour.

Having more time to look at the station the tower of the Bell Rock was a study in how every nook and cranny was utilised. The only sacred areas were around the safety systems, the fire alarms and sprinklers. It was imperative that nothing impeded their workings.

At a place like the Bell Rock anything that broke the routine was welcome and so it was when the news came that an electrician, Ian Robertson, was arriving to do some necessary work. It was decided that his visit was sufficiently close to the time when routine maintenance was due so he would do the whole lot at the one visit.

Ian arrived at the rock not by any of the ships based in Granton, but with Freddie Marr, a fisherman from North Berwick. The NLB quite often chartered Freddie and his boat to make odd trips to the Bell. It was a lot cheaper than sending a ship with just one man and besides, the ships had their other work to do.

In the lighthouse service all the skilled tradesmen, electricians, mechanics, radio engineers and joiners were given the job description of artificers. It was the name that Stevenson gave to his workforce when the Bell Rock was built and has been used ever since.

While Ian was an electrician he was, like all the other artificers, expected to have more than just one narrow skill. In the summer artificers went out to all lighthouses to do routine work but at other times in the event of a breakdown they had to go at short notice. For maintenance purposes the NLB area of Scotland and the Isle of Man was divided into districts. A team of three engineers, an electrician and a radio engineer looked after each district. The three engineers usually went to stations together because they had most work to do. Rock stations might well have three or four generators, three engines to drive the foghorn and perhaps a donkey engine to haul freight. As well as all that there were the lights themselves and sometimes even the replacement of glass panes. A good team could tackle almost any job that needed doing.

During the winter they spent their time in Edinburgh in the NLB workshop. Various bits and pieces of machinery from lighthouses were reconditioned and made ready to be reinstalled the following summer. Artificers all had to be time-served men but there was no guarantee that they would be working in their own trade.

In the years that followed I met Ian Robertson many times. He was a nice man, but will always be remembered for the ring that he wore on the middle finger of his left hand. He had bought it in an Eastern bazaar and it was an ingenious puzzle. When it was taken off it fell to pieces to form a chain. The trick was to put it back together. Try as I might I never learned. Ian showed me often enough but did not really want to give away the secret and used to do it so fast I could never follow what he did. I have seen similar rings since but never one so well made.

This second two-week spell on the Bell Rock seemed a lot shorter than the first. I was far more relaxed and the company was far better. Just as I began to wonder where I might be going next Mr Dickson came on the VHF radio and wanted to speak to me. What he had to say was more than a little interesting.

CHAPTER 18

CRISIS ON MUCKLE FLUGGA

FIRST of all I was to go back to Muckle Flugga. That was exciting enough in itself, but I was going there because there had been a medical emergency. Sandy Wylie had been taken ill. He had been evacuated by helicopter and taken to hospital suffering from severe vomiting and a very high temperature.

It was the first time a helicopter had been used at Flugga. There was no helicopter pad and no place to land. Sandy had to be winched up and Jimmy Andrew Sinclair lowered down to replace him. Little did I know that when a helicopter pad was built at Muckle Flugga I would have quite a big part to play in it. Mr Dickson instructed me to proceed to Unst as quickly as possible. I was to catch the overnight train that went through Waverley Station in the small hours of the morning, go to Aberdeen and fly to Shetland the same day. Tickets, he said, would be ready for me at the check-in desk.

The relief day was cold and blustery and the tide, at the Bell, would be right in the late afternoon. We rigged the mooring ropes on the Fairway landing, knee deep in water but with the tide ebbing fast. It was the *Pharos* that made the relief. Jock Torbet and I were going ashore with John McWilliam remaining on the rock.

When the launch arrived from the ship the state of the tide was just right. With typical decisiveness Mr Swanson came straight in and the boat was tied up without any delay. As well as Jock and myself there was a cargo net full of empty boxes and gas bottles in the boat. It formed a large lump over which a seaman was slumped with the bored air of one who had seen it all before – until, that is, the boat struck the side of the ship and stopped dead. We all got a bit of a shock but this man, totally unprepared, somersaulted over the cargo and became wedged between it and the side of the boat. There he was stuck fast, his welly boats waving in the air. Two of his shipmates hauled him out and back on his feet again. He was cursing a good deal and was laughed at a lot but was none the worse for his mishap. Part of the reason for the crash was the nasty swell that was running. The launch was careering up and down the ship's side about ten feet from trough to crest and getting safely onboard was difficult. Each man had to time his transfer on to the Jacob's ladder, too soon and you risked getting legs and feet crushed, too late and you missed your chance. Any perceived dithering caused shouts of criticism, abuse even. We got onboard just in time for tea and the difference in mood and atmosphere was very noticeable compared with the outward journey. Everyone was in high spirits.

I was pleased to be ashore but had my journey north to consider. Jock and I shared a taxi to the railway station and, almost immediately, Jock caught a westbound train. I had more than six hours to kill; my train was due at 2.30am. I bought a ticket, a newspaper and a paperback book and settled down to wait. Some time after 11pm I began to notice that the waiting room was filling with some of Edinburgh's less favoured citizens. About a dozen tramps came in and crowded around me until I was very uncomfortable. They were dirty, smelly and getting ever bolder and it seemed that the waiting room was the place where they intended to spend the night. I kept my kitbag and grip close to me and tried to ignore them but it was easier said than done. I got really worried about the situation when four policemen, a sergeant and three constables, appeared at the door.

"Right," shouted the Sergeant. "Everybody out!"

He was a huge man and looked, for all the world, like a man used to being obeyed

Slowly and grudgingly the tramps responded and when they were at the door the sergeant turned to me. "You too. Out."

I explained that I was waiting for a train and had every right to be in the waiting room. Intimidating as he was I decided he was less of a threat than the tramps so I refused to go. The sergeant was unmoved.

"Sorry, but our orders are to clear the waiting room and lock it up at midnight."

I did not fancy my chances among the tramps. I told the sergeant that what I had with me was just about all my worldly possessions and I had a month's pay in cash in my wallet. I had no doubt in my mind that the tramps would take everything from me. Although they had been ordered to clear off they were lurking in the shadows waiting for the police to go away. The sergeant's attitude softened for the first time. I was wearing uniform and could prove that I was who I said I was and could show him the ticket for the train.

"OK," he said. "You do have to go out of here but if you wait at the door and if you don't mind being locked up I might be able to help you."

After a time he came back carrying a key and ordered me to follow him. We went to a place on the station where there was little or no lighting. He seemed to know his way and led me to a siding where a railway carriage was parked.

The sergeant explained that the train I was catching picked up this carriage on its way to Aberdeen. It was full of bags of mail and he said, with a grin, that maybe I would find some soft parcels to sleep on.

I climbed up into the mail carriage. The sergeant handed up my luggage and slammed the door shut and I heard the key grating in the lock. It was pitch dark in the carriage but after rummaging around I found a comfortable place to lie. To be locked up was not ideal but if I could not get out then the tramps could not get in. With that piece of comforting logic I fell sound asleep.

I was vaguely aware of the carriage being shunted and heard the sound of the train but when I wakened fully it was daylight and looking out I saw we were just south of Stonehaven. I then made another interesting discovery. A corridor coupled my carriage to the rest of the train and I could walk into the passenger compartments.

My night had been reasonably comfortable but when I got to Aberdeen I felt the need for a wash as well as food. I put my kitbag in the left luggage and had a shower in the station before going to a barber's shop where a man with a steady hand and an open razor shaved me. I have seen open razors being used. Some of the older men at home used them, but I had never used one and had always done my own shaving. It felt really good for an hour or two and after breakfast I made my way to the airport. The one fly in my ointment that day was the fact that Margaret was in Aberdeen and we had no opportunity to see each other.

When I got to the airport, sure enough, my ticket for the flight to Shetland was there at the desk waiting for me. The NLB office staff were mighty efficient in matters of this kind. The flight to Shetland was on time so I made my way to Yell.

I had been told to go to Muckle Flugga as soon as possible but it was unrealistic to try and get there the same day. I contacted the shore station and spoke to Lowry Edwardson and made arrangements to be there the following morning. I was, therefore, able to stay with my parents overnight. It was good to be home again, albeit for the one night. I crossed to Unst after breakfast and had a taxi meet me at the ferry.

When we got off to Flugga the landing was a lot better than my first one but the derrick had to be used. Jimmy Andrew was there ready to come ashore but the other keeper with him was a stranger to me. The relief was successfully completed and I said hello to the new man. He was Tammie Eunson from Exnaboe, near Sumburgh, and had been stationed at Muckle Flugga for a very short time. There was little opportunity to chat at that moment; we had to gather in the ropes with some urgency because the weather was getting worse by the minute. It proved to be a bit of a struggle, the blind leading the blind. My knowledge of how the ropes were stowed was limited and because Tammie had been there such a short time he knew little more than I did. The coils of the rope had to be exactly the right size. Too small and it became too bulky for the hooks. Too big and the ropes rubbed over the rocks.

Eventually we got it done and made our weary way up the 258 steps to the top of the rock. There I met another new face, Tammie Georgeson from Scalloway. He too was new to Muckle

Flugga. Over the ubiquitous cups of tea I was introduced to my new workmates. Tammie Eunson had been transferred from the Mull of Galloway; in the first part of his time there Jack Ross had been his boss. The fact that I knew Jack gave us an immediate link. Tammie Georgeson had come to Muckle Flugga from Douglas Head in the Isle of Man. I got to wonder which of the two was the man in charge. As it turned out they had been in the service the almost the same length of time but Eunson was the senior by a matter of weeks. I had no difficulty in settling in and had not forgotten what I had learned on my first visit.

I asked about Sandy Wylie. He was a lot better, they were pleased to tell me. In fact he was on the mend by the time he left the rock. It was expected that he would soon be back at work. Nonetheless, he had been sent to Aberdeen for tests as a precautionary measure.

For a few days Muckle Flugga was a peaceful place but the news came that the artificers were to arrive for the routine maintenance. They usually came to Muckle Flugga first and visited the other Shetland stations afterwards. It made good sense because Muckle Flugga was the most weather dependent.

When the news came that the *Grace Darling* had left the shore station, the Ness as it was known locally, Tammie Georgeson and I made our way to the landing area, the Comb. What followed was not out of the textbook. The standard of rope handling was poor, to say the least, and it was all down to inexperience.

I did not know enough about rigging the bow rope and the breast rope to prepare them; the one man always worked those two ropes. The stern rope was considered so important that the other man had that and that alone to concentrate on. On this particular day I was given that responsibility while Tammie took the two.

On my first visit it had been drummed into me how important it was to throw the heaving line into the hands of the boatman on the stern rope. One of the tricks of the trade was to soak the heaving line in the sea before the boat arrived. The wet made the line heavier and less likely to be blown off target. All this I did but in my nervousness and anxiety I threw the heaving line too soon and it only just reached the safe hands of Bertie Mathieson in the stern. I was mighty relieved to see him haul in the heavy rope and make it fast. Behind me, when I looked round, Tammie was not nearly so lucky. He had done everything wrong. He had the heaving line for the bow rope over the breast rope so that when the breast rope was tightened it pulled the bow rope out of the hands of the man who was trying to make it fast. If that was not bad enough he had been standing on the wrong side of the ropes and almost got pulled into the sea.

When the cargo hoist was lowered down Tammie Eunson, driving the winch at the top, did not remember to disengage the clutch and with no weight on the hook it refused to lower into the boat but instead tangled tantalizingly just out of reach. I, like a fool, made a joke that they would reach it at high tide. To say that Lowry Edwardson and the crew were not amused was to put it very mildly but to put the tin hat on the whole debacle A. Scott Tulloch, the principal, was in the *Grace Darling* acting as crew because they were a man short. What he said was well into the unprintable category.

Tivvies, as artificers were known, usually hunted in packs of three but on this occasion there were just two of them. John Robson was a man of medium build and red hair. With the derrick it was easy enough to land him. He took hold of the short ladder, released the harness and joined Tammie and I on the Comb. The other man, George Hogarth, was a totally different kettle of fish. He was no more than average height but weighed 22 stone and I wondered if the rope harness would be long enough to go around his enormous girth. It did, just, and the three of us pulling what we were able managed to land him on the Comb.

I think that George was very conscious of his size. Certainly he was somewhat on the defensive, and it would have taken a brave man to make any joke about it. It seems he had tried very hard to lose weight but not when he was on Muckle Flugga. He ate like a horse. I was the cook and huge amounts of food disappeared while he was there. John Robson proved himself to be a dab hand at making doughrings. He volunteered so I gave him all the ingredients he needed and acted as assistant. The doughrings were scoffed as fast as he could make them and by the time that he was finished he had precious few for himself.

George could be a bit cranky sometimes and expressed some strong political views. It seemed that he favoured some ultra-right-wing party. I have my own political views but the kitchen of a rock lighthouse is not the place to pontificate on them.

John Robson was very much at home in Shetland. His wife came from Nesting and as well as being in Shetland because of his work they came, as a family, for holidays and he knew all the Shetland lighthouses and many Shetland folk.

I was glad when Tammie Georgeson took over from me as cook. It was stressful for me cooking for tivvies as well as the keepers and quite often the cook had more work to do than anyone at a rock. Each day Tammie Eunson and I were out working, but the truth was that we did not do much. It was the usual practice for lightkeepers to act as labourers for the tivvies but Tammie kept well out of their way and that suited me because the jobs they gave us to do were never the best. It was cleaning up, scraping carbon off engine parts and gathering up tools that had been scattered around the engine room.

The artificers got through their work despite the fact that they got little help from the lightkeepers and were ready to go ashore at the mid-relief. Going ashore too was Tammie Georgeson. I was to stay along with Tammie Eunson. Tammie Georgeson spent all his spare time painting. He always had an easel set up. His pictures were very attractive and he had a liking for landscapes. Later he was to become a professional artist but in those days it was an enjoyable hobby. Around the kitchen and sitting room at Muckle Flugga there were many examples of his fine work.

It was during this stint on Muckle Flugga that I committed a cardinal sin. The weather was good so it was seen as an opportunity to take on water. Fresh water came in large plastic barrels that held about forty gallons. They were filled at the shore station and taken off by the *Grace Darling*. Landing the water on the rock went without a hitch. The water was emptied into the underground tanks to be pumped to the glass-fibre tanks in the base of the tower, the quarterdeck. The trouble came when we tried to put the empty barrels back down to the boat. I was entrusted with the job of making up the slings. In each sling were six barrels – three at the bottom, two on top of that and one to finish the pyramid. The empty barrels were light and slippery and difficult to stack. In the end I got a sling

Muckle Flugga. © Kieran Murray

around them and put the bight over the hook. The sling was far too long and far too slack, so that the barrels rested on the edge of the cargo platform taking the weight off the sling. It went completely slack and the barrels all spilled out and went, with a noise like thunder, careering down the two hundred foot cliff and into the sea, scattering in all direction.

The boat had to cast off from the landing and retrieve them all. I knew how severe Lowry was about silly mistakes. He was never one to suffer fools gladly. Although I was well out of earshot I could imagine, all too well, what he was saying about my appearance, my intelligence and my parentage. It was another lesson learned.

This mid-relief was a bit out of the ordinary because landing on the rock was the principal keeper, Alex Tulloch, and Sandy Wylie. For the first and only time in my career I was on a rock with three other men. Sandy had been declared fit after his illness and I could only assume I was not needed anywhere else.

Alex was not at all pleased with how he found things. There were a number of jobs he thought should have been done while he was ashore. Of course the visit of the tivvies was blamed but this cut no ice with Alex. We all had to turn out and put everything to rights. We even worked outside on the Sunday. This was highly unusual but Alex felt that the fuel tanks had to be filled. All the diesel oil came in barrels and the barrels were decanted into the tanks as and when they could hold it. It was on that Sunday that an old enemy of mine raised its ugly head again.

For years I had suffered, and suffered is the word, bouts of gout, which is caused by acid crystals forming in the joints. In my case it was my big toe and sometimes my ankle. The pain caused by gout is all but unbearable but there was no way I was going to tell Alex about it. When I made my application to become a lightkeeper I had avoided the question. While I did not tell an out-and-out lie I was evasive, to say the least. In for a penny, in for a pound, as they say. I told Alex another untruth. I told him that a full barrel of diesel had run over my foot and this was what caused the severe pain. For a time he considered sending me ashore but I kept assuring him it was getting better every day. The attack followed the usual pattern and the pain and the swelling did subside after a few days and I could work in comfort again. Muckle Flugga was no place for wounded soldiers and if I had been sent ashore I could hardly grumble.

Having four men on the rock was a real luxury. It gave us four hours on and twelve off, and the only man to have more work was the cook.

All good things come to an end and I knew I would be leaving the Flugga at the next relief. As always, I was eager to know what Mr Dickson had in store for me next. I did not have long to wait.

CHAPTER 19

THE LONGEST JOURNEY

WHEN the word came I was told to proceed to the Calf of Man. I made a mental note that Muckle Flugga was the most northerly station in the NLB area and the Calf of Man the most southerly. The Calf, which had been built to replace the burnt-out Chicken Rock, was flagged up as one of the most modern stations in the service.

Chicken Rock had been a pillar lighthouse completely covered by the high tide. Before restoring the ruin of the old lighthouse the lighthouse board had sent down divers to assess the strength of the rock for long-term viability. They discovered, to their amazement, that the Chicken Rock was like a wine glass or a mushroom. The top part where the base of the tower stood was the biggest area of rock. Underneath the sea it tapered away to a very slender column that looked to be fragile and unsafe so it was considered unwise to retain it as a major lighthouse with men on it.

An automatic, minor, light replaced the main light on the Chicken Rock and a new, state of the art, major light was built on the island, the Calf of Man. I had heard about this new light and it was considered an attractive posting.

I was quite excited about going to the Isle of Man and something entirely new. Mr Dickson gave me travel instructions. I was to fly from Sumburgh on the Saturday to Glasgow and spend the night there. I reached Glasgow Airport without incident but had the problem of finding somewhere to spend the night. I decided to take a bus into the city centre and look around for accommodation.

While I was waiting a man, a total stranger, came and offered me a lift. I ignored him. I suspected his motives and wanted nothing to do with him. After about five minutes he was back repeating the offer, but I did not accept. He came back a third time and said this was my last chance as he was going. I asked him who he was and why was he offering to help me. He explained that he was a bus driver who had been sent to pick up twenty-four Norwegians, the crew of a ship. In the event only nine of them had arrived so he had plenty of room in his bus so if I wanted to come with them I was welcome. I asked him if he had any advice to give me as to where I could stay the night. He replied that I should stay with the Norwegians because the hotel they were booked into was bound to have spare capacity. This I did and spent a very comfortable night at a modest cost.

The following day I made my way to the airport but the flight to the Isle of Man was not until the afternoon. We went by way of Belfast and, for the first time, I had a first-hand encounter with the security services there. When we landed at Aldergrove it was raining heavily. We were escorted to the terminal building and told to wait until our luggage was ready for collection. Everyone's luggage was deposited on an open piece of tarmac and we were told to collect what belonged to each of us. I had a brand new, blue, suitcase that had no label on it. When I saw what I thought was my case I could not take it because it had a white sticky label plastered on the flat side of it. Fellow passengers filed past me and picked up their cases and bags and I had to stand in the pouring rain waiting and hoping that my case, without a label, would appear.

Eventually only the one case remained and my discomfort and uncertainty was noticed by a security guard. I explained my problem but he had little sympathy. I asked him if I could check it to see whether it was mine.

"Take it if it's yours," he said. "Otherwise don't go near it."

I asked him what would happen to it if I did not claim it.

"We'll blow it up!"

I ventured a little nearer and had a flash of inspiration. I remembered that my case, new though it was, had a scrub mark on the corner. This case had the same mark so I took my courage in both hands and claimed it. I can only assume that the label had been detached from another item of luggage by the rain. The security man was unconcerned. The fact that I had taken the case meant that it ceased to be a problem for him.

After a short wait I boarded an aircraft bound for the Isle of Man. Mr Dickson had told me that, on arrival at Ronaldsway, I was to look out for John Gawn. John was the boatman at the Calf and was to take me to the guesthouse in Port St Mary where I was to spend the night. The airport was quiet and soon all the passengers from my flight had dispersed and I pretty much had the place to myself. There was no sign of John Gawn or anyone who may have come in his place. In the lighthouse service the promise of being met did not always happen.

Over time my patience wore thin and I looked through my notes to see if I had a phone number for the station or the shore station but I could find nothing. I approached a taxi driver and asked how much it would cost to hire him to take me to Port St Mary.

"Nothing at all," he answered. "You boys in the services do a great job and I am pleased to help in any way I can."

I told him that I was willing to pay him his fare but he would not hear of it. He told me that he knew John Gawn and that he was very forgetful. He took me to John Gawn's house and there he was, working in his garden.

John was quick to apologise. He had, as the taxi driver suggested, completely forgotten he had been told to pick me up at the airport. I thanked the taxi man for his kindness and John invited me in for a cup of tea. He had remembered to book me into the guesthouse of Mrs Schofield. All lighthouse personnel stayed with Mrs Schofield, who had a nice place and gave me an attractive meal of gammon and pineapple, which I enjoyed greatly. I arranged to have breakfast at eight in the morning. John said he would pick me up at 8.45.

John used his own boat. The reliefs at the lighthouse were something of a sideline for him; he was semi-retired but earned money as a fisherman. His boat was sleek and fast and the trip to the Calf seemed to take no time at all. Soon we were tied up at the jetty and I was met by the keeper going ashore and the man who was to be my boss for the next two weeks. He was a stout bald-headed man whose hair, when he had any, had been red. His name was Harry Quirk and he was a Manxman born and bred. When we got to the lighthouse I met the third man, Jimmy Jackson. Jimmy was from Lancashire originally but had been drawn to the Isle of Man because of his love of motorcycles. As a young man he saved up his money all year so that he could go to the island to watch the famous Tourist Trophy races. In those days the races, held every summer, were the pinnacle, the Mecca, for the best motorbike riders in the world. Equally famous machines like Rudge, AJS and most of all Norton took part annually.

By the 1970s the TT races had lost something of their dominance in the world of motorcycle racing. Foreign manufacturers made multi-cylinder machines that were faster than British bikes. MV Agusta, Gilera and Moto Guzzi from Italy became the bikes that won all the races in the late '50s and '60s and the best British riders, like Geoff Duke and John Surtees, signed lucrative contracts to ride them to success after success. Later, Japanese motorbikes appeared and Honda and Yamaha became household names. The new generation of racers became faster every year and the safety of riders caused great concern. Some of the top performers considered the 37.5 mile Manx circuit so dangerous they did not want to compete.

In 1957 the first 100mph lap was recorded and into the 1960s races had an average speed of more than 100mph. The world championship events were now held at Grand Prix circuits but, nonetheless, motorcycle enthusiasts still came to the Isle of Man in their hundreds to enjoy a fabulous week of their favourite sport.

Jimmy had eventually moved to the island and made his home there. He was the occasional lightkeeper at the Calf and earned useful money to eke out his retirement pension.

When I had time to look around the station was, indeed, very modern. The light was fundamentally different from any I had seen before. It took the form of a bank of sealed beams, rather like the floodlights at a football stadium or, more simply, twenty car headlights set close together in a square. The whole lot revolved and the cleverest bit of the mechanism was the way electricity was transmitted through the movement.

Straightforward wiring was not an option because the cable would twist up. There had to be a swivel. The current was conducted through the shaft on which the light turned. A separate circuit served the emergency light, which was more sealed beams around two sides of the main bank of lights. An electric motor caused the bank of lights to revolve, giving the lighthouse its character.

The tower is square and low. Lighthouse architecture had come a long way from the days of the Stevensons. Each lightkeeper had his own bedroom with some extra rooms for tivvies. To have the privacy of a bedroom of one's own was greatly valued by lightkeepers. In an all-male world time spent alone was quality time to be treasured. Every other lighthouse I had served at had been old, but the Calf of Man was new and modern in every aspect.

The whole island was a nature reserve and every living thing was protected. Neither lightkeepers nor anyone visiting killed anything, not even an insect, outdoors. Roaming around were the Manx sheep. They looked a lot like Shetland sheep except they had four horns and, for me, were something of a novelty. It was May and the young lambs were frolicking in the sunshine.

Every day there was a stiff breeze and in the shade it felt cold, but out of the wind it was pleasantly warm. While I was there I spent most of my time outdoors because Harry was preparing for the annual inspection. I was given the job of cleaning and tidying the path to the fog signal. A narrow ditch at each side of the path was wanted and the grass had to be cut too. The weather was great for working outside, bright and breezy. I worked at that every day and for the first time in my life got a proper suntan. The combination of wind and sun made all exposed skin a rich brown colour. It also worked up a healthy appetite and here, I am sorry to say, came the bitter bit. Food, on the Calf of Man, was a scarce commodity.

Jimmy Jackson was the cook and the portions he dished up to each of us were derisory. One day we had fish fingers for dinner, two of them, and I could count, at a glance, the number of peas, seven of them, and the chips were huddled together in one pathetic mouthful. Bread was rationed to one slice per man in the mornings with a spot of porridge. I made a resolution that when I became cook there would be big changes, but on this I was second-guessed and told firmly exactly what I was allowed to cook, so my meals turned as frugal as Jimmy's.

The only time that I saw a decent meal was the day of the annual inspection. A bit of a show was put on for the benefit of the superintendent. That said, it was not the sort of meal that would give anyone a fatty heart or put the cholesterol levels off the scale but it was the best on offer during my stay there. At all other times I went around hungry.

It was the first, and thankfully, the only rock station where I experienced this problem. There was no excuse for it and the only reason for skimping on food was to have surplus money for sharing out among the keepers. At another station, in the past, keepers had had to be treated for malnutrition because they were too stingy to feed themselves. The NLB took an extremely dim view of this given that they provided an adequate sustenance allowance along with freezer space and emergency rations.

Also on the Calf was a senior artificer and he too suffered from hunger. He used to get up in the middle of the night if he knew I was on watch. I could give him a cup of tea but there was not much else and if any biscuits went missing out of the tin that would have been noticed. The tivvy strongly suggested that

I should complain but I told him I would not. I was on a hiding to nothing. I was still on probation and did not want to leave the Calf of Man with a bad report. If he, as a senior engineer, had made a strong complaint it would have carried weight, but as a lowly Super I had no chance. In any case I knew that I would soon be on the move again and more, and better, food would be mine again.

As it turned out I was there for rather less than two weeks. Mr Dickson came on the phone and I was told to proceed once again to Rubh Ré. On the morning I was to go ashore the weather was marginal with strong winds and waves crashing over the jetty. We spoke to John Gawn and told him of the conditions but he decided he would have a look at it. I packed up all my gear and made ready for the shore but without too much hope of leaving the Calf. However, the wind died down and after some delay the boat came into the jetty, my replacement stepped off and I got into the boat.

I had enjoyed my trip to the Calf of Man despite the poor feeding. The weather had been good, I had been outdoors all the time and I knew that the chances of being there again were slim. It was yet another opportunity that had come through my employment in the lighthouse service.

Back at Port St Mary I went back to the same guesthouse. Mrs Schofield made me welcome to stay the night as it was, by this time, too late in the day to leave the island. My flight out was booked for the following day, Sunday.

Having left the Calf of Man my first and foremost priority was food. A delicious smell of fried fish came from a chip shop and I homed in on that like a bloodhound. A fish supper was a generous portion and the taste every bit as good as the smell. It was scoffed in a matter of moments. However, nice as it was, it did little to satisfy the hunger that had intensified day by day at the lighthouse so I went back to the shop and bought another one. After eating that I decided that I would manage without any more food until dinnertime.

I had a walk around Port St Mary. It proved to be a quiet, pleasant and charming place. Manx folk were rather cosmopolitan insofar as they were used to seeing people from throughout Britain and beyond. In some places in England shopkeepers are unwilling to accept Scottish banknotes but in the Isle of Man they will take whatever kind of money is offered. One shopkeeper asked me if I had ever seen a Manx cat. When I said no he said they had one as a pet and offered to show it to me. This proved to be easier said than done and by the time he accepted that the cat was nowhere to be found I was fed up with the whole idea and cared not if the wretched animal had two tails or none.

CHAPTER 20

BACK BY BELFAST

THE short flight to Belfast was mid-morning and I had rather a long wait for the connecting flight to Glasgow. Unaccustomed as I was to the security in the airport it was quite obvious that something out of the ordinary was taking place. The whole area was swarming with troops armed to the teeth. Most of them looked too young to grow a beard. They looked like schoolboys.

To leave luggage unattended, even for a second, was to lose it. The soldiers came every few minutes and looked under all the seats. Passengers had to have all baggage out in the open and the muzzles of rifles were passed under the seats to ensure nothing was concealed there. I was mighty glad when the time came to board the aircraft and get out of this highly charged, tense atmosphere. That night, when I heard the news on the TV, I understood why Aldergrove was so tense; it had been the worst day of violence in the province since the infamous Bloody Sunday in Derry some months previously.

Although I had left the Calf of Man at short notice there was no great urgency in getting to Rubh Ré. I was given leave to go to Aberdeen and see Margaret. It would have been nice to fly all the way but there were limits to the generosity of the NLB's travel allowances so I made my way to Queen Street railway station and caught a train north.

Although I had had plenty of food since leaving the Calf of Man the legacy of that hungry time lingered. It was now mid-afternoon and I had not eaten since breakfast. There had been no opportunity in Belfast to eat and I was distinctly peckish. I made my way to the buffet car and bought a packet of sandwiches and a cup of coffee. When I sat down at a table I was immediately joined by another man who was also wearing a uniform. He told me his name was Bert Eddy and that he was second officer on a ship that had docked in Glasgow. He was going home on shore leave. When I spoke to him he clocked my accent at once. He knew I came from Shetland.

It turned out that we had a lot of mutual acquaintances. In his time he had had many Shetland shipmates, one of them being Margaret's brother-in-law. He then asked me where I was going so I told him that I was going to Aberdeen to see my fiancée. He then asked me another question.

"Where does she stay?"

I explained that she shared a flat with another girl in Lamond Place.

"It's off Jamaica Street," I went on.

Bert seemed to find this quite amusing. When I asked him what he was laughing at he said: "I live in Jamaica Street, and what's more my wife will meet me at the railway station so we can give you a lift up the road."

Right enough Mrs Eddy was there with the family car, a VW Beetle. It was a bit of a crush to get all the baggage stowed but I was soon in Lamond Place.

Margaret saw my arrival and came out to meet me. She gave me a kiss but her welcome, to my dismay, lacked somewhat in warmth. I could not think why. After all, absence is supposed to make the heart grow fonder. Clearly the old adage was wrong.

Inside the flat Stella Caithness, Margaret's flatmate, greeted me and after a conversion that did not flow Margaret revealed her concern.

"Where on earth have you been that you could not get a wash?"

I burst out laughing. It was the first time that she had ever seen me with a suntan. She thought I had a dirty face and no doubt wondered what the rest of me was like.

CHAPTER 21

PLANNING THE FUTURE

I STAYED in the flat with Margaret and Stella, risky though this was. If the landlord had known that a man was staying in the flat he would have been very angry. If the college had known, it would have been unacceptable to them as well. I kept a low profile and no-one was any the wiser.

This leave was as welcome as it was unexpected and it gave Margaret and I a golden opportunity not only to be together but also to try and plan our wedding. We always planned to get married during 1972 when Margaret was finished at college. However, setting a date was far from easy.

I knew I had made some progress up the seniority list of supernumeraries but had no idea when I might be appointed. I had asked Mr Dickson if I could have leave to allow me to get married but he was somewhat dismissive. He said that it was too far ahead and to ask him nearer the time.

It was now the middle of May and we had to find a date that would suit our families as well as everyone else. We could have had a very quiet wedding with only our nearest and dearest attending but we both had our hearts set on a traditional Shetland wedding, two nights and two hundred or more guests.

Margaret's father and brothers, along with the rest of the Cullivoe Fiddlers, were invited to play in the Kinross Folk Festival so we had to avoid those dates. They all made their living in crofting and farming so, equally, we had to avoid harvest time. After a lot of thought we settled on 5th October. This could only be a provisional date at best. There were so many uncertainties and I still had no promise of leave but it was the best we could do. We still had to consult our families and check that we were not clashing with any important event already arranged at home.

With the optimism of young people in love we went to a jeweller's in Aberdeen city centre to buy wedding rings. We did quite a lot of window-shopping before venturing into any shop. Margaret immediately fell in love with a fairly broad gold band that was different because the edges were scalloped, so her choice was easy. Weddings rings are forever and I picked mine carefully. It is a broad, plain gold ring that I have enjoyed wearing ever since.

We also discussed other aspects of the big day and although we knew who we wanted as the best man and bridesmaid they, too, had to be contacted. Margaret's brother was my choice as best man. He had done this job for others before and was as yet unmarried. The bridesmaid was to be my cousin Elizabeth.

Leave flew past as always and I made my way, yet again, to the West Highlands and Rubh Ré, determined to approach Mr Dickson at the first opportunity regarding marriage leave. At Rubh Ré nothing much had changed but the whole station looked clean and fresh.

It was the first time I had been there in summer and it was typical of Jack Ross that he had started the painting and summer work early. Most of it was done. The tower had been lime washed and all the doors and windows had been painted. Even the dome was newly painted, much to my relief.

Grass cutting was an on-going job and there was a considerable amount of tidying to be completed. Many another principal lightkeeper would have accepted the station as it was but Jack wanted everything in apple-pie order for the forthcoming inspection. In this regard I felt a little hard done by. I had just left an inspection at the Calf of Man.

One of the things Jack wanted rid of was an old car that some previous lightkeeper had left behind. It was well past any use or repair and he announced that we would dump it over the cliff. Using the station car we towed it up the hill. From there it was a straight run down to the shore, about three hundred yards down a smooth hill. We man-handled it off the road and pointed it in the direction we wanted it to go in. Jack was shouting loudly for everyone to stand well clear. He was scared that any of us got our clothes caught and were dragged down the hill by the car when we let it go. Down the hill it went straight as a dye and gathered speed all the way until it disappeared and we heard the crash as it hit the rocks below.

Inspection day passed without incident. The ship carrying the stores and the superintendent was the *Fingal*. The landing stage at Rubh Ré was some distance from the station. The diesel oil for engines that powered the fog signal and the paraffin for the light came in fifty-gallon steel barrels and had to be transported to the station by one means or another. There was a pipeline and a pump but it all looked to be in poor order with clear signs of rust and corrosion on the pipe. Jack decided to give it a try but in the end it made for more work rather than less. We emptied two barrels into the feeder tank at the landing and, after a struggle during which the phrase "pump priming" came to mind, we got the pump working. However, when we walked along the pipeline the many leaks told us that little or no diesel would ever reach the station. We therefore had to try and salvage what we could from the pipe and the feeder tank and get it back into the barrels.

Rubh Ré had no tractor; the station car was a Morris 1100 and was never designed for haulage work. In the end we had to do it the hard way. Each man took a barrel and rolled it along the road all the way to the lighthouse. Fortunately the road is relatively flat with just the one difficult, steep part near the landing. Nonetheless it was back-breaking work and we were all mighty relieved when the last of the barrels was inside the lighthouse gates.

The business of rolling barrels was good for working up an appetite, not that my appetite needed much encouragement. When we were in Gairloch buying the weekly stores I saw beautiful looking lamb in the window of the butcher's shop. It was a scandalous price but it looked so good that I bought a leg. The following morning I was on the 6am watch so I decided to roast the lamb. My thinking was that it would save me time at night. When I came back to the bothy for breakfast the meat smelt delicious so I tasted a bit. It was so good and I was so hungry that I ate the whole lot there and then. When I bought it I believed it would be two dinners for me but it never got beyond one breakfast.

During this stint at Rubh Ré I had a slight accident. I fell over the cliff. Jack was having another purge of unwanted debris and was going to burn a pile of old rotten wood. Some of it had fallen over the edge and down on the beach. I was going to climb down to get it when I slipped and fell. Thankfully the cliff there was not high but, instinctively, I made a grab with my left hand and caught my engagement ring on the fence. When I landed on the shingle my first thought was to try and assess how much damage I had done. However, a more powerful concern was the beautiful onyx ring that Margaret had given me with a loving kiss. Pain was manifesting itself in many parts of my body but the ring finger very sore indeed. The finger was bleeding and the ring was twisted almost into a figure eight. I feared that my finger might be broken or dislocated but it was just cut and sore. I got to my feet to find that everything worked.

I developed some interesting bruises. My body was all colours of the rainbow but I had no lasting hurts. As for the ring, we had a tough job getting it off my finger. I would not allow Jack to cut it. I reshaped it but it was never quite the same. I still have it, although I do not wear it any more.

All during this time I spoke to Margaret and to my parents daily. It seemed that 5th October was a suitable day for our wedding. It was now a case of me getting leave and us telling everyone that needed to know. Of course there were all the arrangements to make as well.

I managed to speak to Mr Dickson. I told him we had decided on a date for our wedding. He was much more receptive this time and although he stopped short of promising leave he said he would do his best to arrange leave. With this I had to be content.

CHAPTER 22

FAREWELL TO RUBH RÉ

I HAD now been at Rubh Ré for four weeks and guessed that I would soon be moving on. There was movement in the list of supernumeraries; the most senior Supers had been appointed to stations and ahead of them some senior assistants had been promoted to principals.

It all gave me hope that my turn might come soon but I had to be as patient as I could and take things as they came. I had done three spells of duty at Rubh Ré and while I had been reasonably happy I was ready to leave and it was not a station I would want to be appointed to.

Jack came with the message that Mr Dickson wanted to speak to me. I was hoping against hope that it was news of my appointment but in this I was disappointed. Not only that, but he told me to proceed to the Bell Rock. He did add that I was being sent there because first assistant Len Fraser had been promoted. Another keeper was off sick so they needed a supernumerary who knew the station and did not need training. This made me feel a bit better. I felt needed as I once more packed up my belongings and boarded the bus in Gairloch to catch the train from Kyle of Lochalsh to Inverness at Achnasheen. When the train stopped at the Achnasheen station the passengers left en masse. When I was about to board I was told there was no hurry. The guard went on to explain that the driver had gone into the hotel. He had been at a wedding the night before and was in urgent need of some refreshment.

I instinctively knew that I would not be back at Rubh Ré, at least not as a lightkeeper. I had no great liking for the station but I did have good friends there and wondered if I would ever see them again. One such person was John Thomson, a retired keeper who lived in Gairloch. John was an Orkney man and a treasure trove of stories about lightkeepers and lighthouses.

One story I remember well was of the supernumerary going to Skerryvore when John was the principal lightkeeper. He and the Super were travelling to the rock on the *Fingal*. The weather overhead was fine but recent bad weather had left quite a heavy swell. It was the Super's first time to a rock and John knew it was going to be tricky getting him from the ship into the launch. John sized up his young companion and judged him to be without fear but big and clumsy. He explained the dangers of being crushed between the boat and the ship and advised him to wait until the boat was as high as it was going to get and, forget the ladder, just jump in. This way, John reasoned, even if his boarding was not dignified at least no-one would get hurt. Not so. When the time came the Super had a glance over the side at the boat, put his hand on the ship's rail and vaulted over at entirely the wrong time and landed with both feet on the head and neck of the engine man. In fact the boat was in a deep trough just beginning to rise and the drop from the level of the ship's deck was about twenty feet. The engine man was slumped over the engine cover with the air of one who had seen it all before. That all changed when this fourteen stone man landed on top of him. Such was the impact that his face was squashed down on the cover, breaking his false teeth and giving him a nosebleed.

When John came onboard the engine man was still spitting out bits of his dentures and wiping away blood with a disgusting hanky. Save for one look of utter contempt he totally ignored the Super but turned on John.

"Who is this goddamned eejit that you have brought here?" he shammed.

By now the journey from the West Highlands to Edinburgh was a familiar one. I changed trains in Inverness and, on arrival at Waverley, took a taxi to Granton and joined the *Hesperus*. I was given tea and biscuits and shown a bunk in the lightkeeper's cabin.

Foremost in my mind, as always going to the Bell Rock, was the question of who my companions would be. To find out I had to wait for morning and the time when other keepers joined the ship. Imagine my surprise and pleasure when a weel kent face appeared on board. It was none other than my old mate Charlie Reid, who I had last seen at Rubh Ré many months ago. He too eagerly awaited appointment and had reason to believe his appointment was imminent. I hoped he was right because I knew I was not too far behind him.

Although it was summer it was an extremely unpleasant day weatherwise – heavy drizzle, poor visibility and very cold. The ebb tide was running in the face of a force five to six wind, making the sea choppy, rough even. Neither Charlie nor I had waterproofs. In practice we seldom needed waterproofs and to own a suit was something extra to carry around from station to station. Going to places like the Bell Rock it was always possible to borrow oilskins from the ship. Or so we thought. When we asked for waterproofs we were told abruptly that there were none available. Supernumeraries, they said, had borrowed several suits of waterproofs and never taken them back and they were not prepared to lose any more. They added that we should have had our own.

John McWilliam was there too. The rock was to be cleared, and he added his twopence worth. "If you come to the rock with soaking wet clothes," he said, "don't expect to be able to wash them in fresh water because there is a shortage of water."

Travelling around as we did we carried no more clothes than we needed and could ill afford to have clothes we could neither wash nor wear. Drastic measures were, therefore, called for. We went to the cabin and stripped naked. I put on the thinnest jeans I had and a tee-shirt over bare skin without underwear or socks. Charlie did the same. On arrival at the Bell we got into the launch and it was sod's law that the tide was slow to ebb that day. Soon we were both soaked and the cold began to grip. As well as the steady, heavy drizzle the blunt bows of the launch were butting into the waves causing a deluge of spray to come onboard. It was all I could to stop my teeth clattering and by the time that we got inside the lighthouse we were like drowned rats.

We saw Len Fraser leave the Bell for the last time. He was going ashore to pack up and go to a new station as principal. As soon as we could we rubbed ourselves down with a dry towel and got on dry clothes. Back in the kitchen we had a welcome cup of hot tea. We tentatively suggested that the bottle of brandy was kept especially for men who were wet and cold. This fell on deaf ears so we had to be content with the tea.

Charlie was even more experienced than I was. He had joined the service before me but it was his first time at the Bell so I was given the job of showing him the routine and the workings of the station. We soon settled in and with Charlie and I being old friends we had a lot of fun.

John disapproved of us wrestling on the kitchen floor. He was worried we might injure each other. If this happened he declared that not only he would have to work the station himself but he would have to organise our evacuation from the rock and, to add insult to injury, would be reprimanded for allowing such irresponsible behaviour.

One trick that Charlie played was a bit over the top. It was on a Sunday afternoon and as the man on watch it was my job to make the tea. Charlie and John were in the kitchen too. John had a cup of his own that he drank all his tea and coffee from. It was a small china cup. Delicate and thin, it was little thicker than an eggshell. When I opened the cupboard door John's cup fell out and split in two. Charlie had taken the cup, reached around the central post to which the doors fastened, and propped it against the shut door. I expected John to be angry but he was just hurt. He would not accept any other cup and he went without either tea or coffee for several days. The loss of the cup took on the magnitude of a bereavement. John never found out that Charlie had done this as a prank and, of course, I never told him, but when I got Charlie by himself I called him everything but a gentleman. It passed by and in a few days was forgotten. We began to think about other things.

There was no Norman Wilson to bully Supers out of watching what they wanted to see on TV and as it happened we all wanted to watch the same programme, the Wimbledon Tennis Championships. In those days it was all black and white but it was on every day with a highlights programme at night. We closely followed the fortunes of Yvonne Goolagong, Mrs Cawley and that year, 1972, was the first time the final of the men's singles was played on a Sunday. We eagerly watched Stan Smith play Ilie Nastase in a closely contested match. In the end the powerful American with his cannonball serve overcame the very quick and skilful Romanian.

We were all on tenterhooks wondering what the situation was going to be at the relief. John McWilliam would be staying on the rock to complete his month but would Charlie and I be leaving? We knew that one of us would go because the NLB never had the same three men together on any rock for a whole month. On the other hand the station was seriously undermanned. One lightkeeper had resigned and the other two had been transferred but not yet replaced.

We did not have to wait long to get the answers. Charlie was the one to stay for another two weeks but at the same time came the news of his appointment. He was to leave, pack his effects and proceed to his appointment. There was no firm news of my appointment but I, too, had something to look forward to. Mr Dickson spoke to me in detail about my next assignment, Out Skerries in Shetland. It was not just for the usual few weeks but until the automation of the station was completed in December. I was to have the status of an assistant – that is, two weeks on and two weeks off. Needless to say this was exciting news. Mr Dickson never said so but he clearly implied that appointment would follow. Out Skerries would be my last station as a Super. I was to share this time with Jim Hardie. Jim, from Bressay, was waiting for promotion because he was a senior assistant.

At Out Skerries there were no actual lightkeeping duties but the Board of Trade insisted that a lightkeeping presence was maintained until the automation was complete. The principal keeper was Magnus MacDonald who wanted away because he did not like the upheaval of the contractors' work. In contrast to me he was a senior principal keeper who would retire sooner rather than later. In other words, I was to be a token keeper marking time but, of course, that did not trouble me at all. After more than a year as a supernumerary I had all the experience I needed and was ready to go to any station in the service.

In the meantime, Margaret had graduated from college and was at home waiting for our wedding and for me to be appointed to a lighthouse. The Skerries posting meant I would be at home for two weeks out of four. The outlook was rosy, especially when Mr Dickson said he had not forgotten about my need for wedding leave.

Margaret's joy in graduation was tempered by the fact that many of her college friends had failed. Some of them were organising appeals but it was some of the brightest students who had been given the thumbs down.

CHAPTER 23

OUT SKERRIES

THE rest of my time at the Bell Rock went past in a haze. My head was too full of the events to come that no thought was put into what I was doing. Fortunately I knew the station so well by this time that I had no need for intense concentration, but relief day could never come soon enough.

Mr Dickson phoned again and told me to report to his office before I left Edinburgh. As always on relief day we arrived in Granton far too late. The board's offices had been closed for hours. I stayed overnight, once again, in the YMCA hostel and in the morning went to see Mr Dickson. I am not exactly sure why he wanted to see me but he gave me more instructions and told me more about what I had to do in Skerries.

The old light had been dismantled and a temporary light installed. It was automatic and controlled by a photo-electric cell and therefore needed no attention. However, it was powered by batteries and those batteries had to be charged regularly. My other lightkeeping duty was to do the 'speaks' to Muckle Flugga, Bressay and Lerwick Coastguard. This was routine radio contact that all rock stations kept with each other. At other times I was to work with and help the contractors, T L Arcus, in any way I could.

Mr Dickson also told me that the tower at Out Skerries had been gutted and therefore there was no accommodation on the rock. I was to stay in Skerries, in the community, with the Williamson family at Seaside Cottage. I was to be paid a subsistence allowance and from that I was to pay Mrs Williamson for my keep.

Travel between my home in Yell and Skerries was not entirely straightforward and the journey could not be made in one day. The Skerries link with the outside world was the inter-island steamer *Earl of Zetland*. However, by the time the *Earl* called at Mid Yell it had already been in Skerries so Mr Dickson understood that I had to travel and stay overnight in Lerwick on my way to Skerries.

Just before I left HQ I was given an air ticket to Shetland but first I had to get the train to Aberdeen in order to catch the afternoon flight. All this I managed without incident and eventually I arrived in Lerwick late in the afternoon. Without sparing any expense I hired a taxi and got home in the evening. This gave me a few days home before I had to go to Skerries for the first time. Of course Margaret and I had a joyous reunion and talked non-stop about our wedding plans and making arrangements. All too soon I had to go. I was due in Skerries on the Monday so I had to travel to Lerwick on Sunday night. The *Earl* left Victoria Pier at 8am.

I booked myself into the fishermen's mission and was onboard in good time in the morning. I rather feared the journey because I am somewhat prone to seasickness and the weather was bad, with a gale force south-east wind. The mate on the *Earl* told me the call along Skerries was in some doubt because of the weather. He would not give any definite decision; he said they would make up their minds when we got there.

Before we were out of Lerwick harbour he came back and told me that they had decided to bypass Skerries. The only call to be made was at Whalsay and then on to Mid Yell.

All this meant that I landed back home again but the *Earl* was to call at Mid Yell again at the ungodly hour of 6.30am in the morning and call in at Skerries on the way back to Lerwick. I was on the Mid Yell pier when they arrived. The wind had died down and the landing in Skerries was in no doubt.

It was mid-morning when we steamed in the north mouth of the Skerries harbour. The *Earl* anchored and the flit boat came chugging out to meet us. In those days flit boats were a common sight around the ports where the steamer called. They were used to take people and goods ashore in places without a pier or where the water was too shallow at low tide to allow berthing. This was to be the only time that I met Magnus MacDonald. He boarded the *Earl* from the flit boat, we shook hands, and I stepped into the flit boat from the low waist of the *Earl*. At the pier I was met and shown to Seaside Cottage and into the home of the Williamson family, into a house full of kindness and hospitality.

I was not expected to go to the Bound Skerry where the lighthouse was. It was my first day and I was given the afternoon to settle in. That I did. My bedroom was directly above the kitchen and was warm and comfortable.

The Williamsons were a large family. The man of the house was Arthur, a semi-retired fisherman. He had been skipper of a very well-known fishing boat, the *Swiftwing*. Now the *Swiftwing* was used as a cargo boat and ran to and from Vidlin on the Shetland mainland. As I was to learn, Arthur sometimes

Out Skerries lighthouse. © *Kieran Murray* ➤

skippered her still. Maggie, his wife, was a kind, generous lady who made sure everyone was well fed. Their son Magnie was home all the time. He worked at the fish factory. Another son, Cecil, was home some of the time and the youngest of the family, Stewart, was working at building the new pier. Sons Tom and Duncan lived in Lerwick while John was married and lived in Nesting. They also had two daughters who lived in Lerwick. The whole house seemed to be alive with people, always coming and going. From the start I felt welcome and soon became part of the household.

For my first day at the lighthouse I joined the relief boat with Bobby Johnson in charge. His crew was Archie Williamson, a cousin of Arthur's, Donnie Henderson and Andrew Anderson. Also in the boat was Jimmy Sandison, the works foreman, and his team.

Donnie had been the occasional keeper when the lighthouse was conventional and it was with him that I spent my time. He showed me what little there was to see at the station and told me what we had to do in the way of lightkeeping duties. It was, more or less, what Mr Dickson had told me.

However, there was a little more. We all had packed lunches but we boiled a kettle on a gas ring and made tea at break times. Donnie had his own boat and every day he and I went to the shop. All the men took turns at buying the tea, sugar, milk and biscuits, etc. Some of us smoked while others chewed gum and ate sweets. Each morning a list of requirements was compiled and a note of how much money each man had given us so that we could give back the correct change.

Donnie had an outboard motor on his boat and I came to love our trips ashore. George William Henderson's shop was like an Aladdin's cave. He had everything that anyone would ever want to buy. Skerries had no petrol pump, which is hardly surprising when you consider that there is only 1km of road. Petrol, with white spirit, paraffin, diesel, coal tar, sheep dip and linseed oil, was all kept in five-gallon drums in the store of the shop.

Once when George William was away on holiday in Edinburgh a mistake was made with the drums. Andrew John, George William's father, put five gallons of white spirit in the minister's car instead of petrol. When I asked what happened Andrew calmly replied: "Shö güd ower weel bit shö reeked a coarn!"

George also had, in his shop, a record library. A long, broad shelf was full of long-playing records. The selection was varied but, as you might expect, there was an emphasis on traditional music and country and western. It cost £2 to hire an album for a week and another £2 to buy it outright if you liked it enough.

Our trips ashore were never hurried. Sometimes Donnie would check up on his lobster creels so a big slice of every morning was very pleasantly spent. From my point of view I met many of the local folk at the shop and got to know them.

Skerries is the warmest, kindest, most welcoming community that I know. Everyone I met invited me to visit and they all went out of their way to make me feel at home. When I went there first I knew only one person. She was the district nurse, Marie Mann. Marie had been a schoolmate at Mid Yell. She was one of the most popular girls in the school. Her father was a Yell man, from the Herra, who had been a lightkeeper and her mother came from Lewis. She was soon to marry a Skerries man and become Mrs Tom Henry Anderson.

Links between Skerries and North Yell were nothing new. I remember Skerries fishing boats being regular visitors at the Cullivoe pier. Cullivoe was convenient for whitefish boats. Not only was it a safe place but it was close to the rich fishing grounds to the north of Yell. The Cullivoe fishermen and their wives and girlfriends were always invited to the weddings in Skerries. The islands had suffered depopulation and there were hardly enough folk in Skerries to hold a really lively, traditional wedding that lasted several days.

By the time I started at the Skerries lighthouse the work was well advanced. The tower was gutted and the beautiful lens, through which the light was magnified, had been dismantled and thrown over the balcony to smash to smithereens on the rocks below. I always felt, and still feel, that this was a dreadful act of vandalism, but looking at it in the cold light of day there was not much that could be done with it. It had done its job, had its day, and was no more use. However, to make something like it today to that standard of precision would cost a fortune. I had to content myself with gathering up a few fragments of glass that was once part of a complex prism weighing over two tons. I also found a roller, which had acted as a stabilizer for the lens as it floated in the mercury bath. I looked on them as being rather sad souvenirs but I took them home anyway. It did not mean anything to the folk at home and they were somewhat less than impressed.

High on the tower was the temporary light. It was about the size of a small barrel and required no attention except that the batteries that powered it had to be recharged regularly. For this we had a small generator which ran on petrol, but this did not have to be used every day. After all, it was the height of summer and the light was exhibited for a short time each night.

The tower itself looked very smart. It had been lime washed, as were all lighthouses, but for the automation it had had a makeover. All the old lime, and indeed the blackening from the wartime regulations, had been sandblasted off and it had been painted with several coats of snow white, waterproof emulsion paint. After all the lining from inside the tower had been stripped away the walls had been sealed and likewise painted. In an automatic lighthouse the policy was to eliminate everything combustible to avoid any question of fire. The new permanent light would run on gas and many bottles of gas had to be stored in the tower. A fire in such a tower could cause the gas to explode, and if this happened the whole structure would probably be damaged beyond repair. Another reason for having the walls bare was to leave no place where insects could breed. Flying insects caused havoc in automatic lights. Attracted by the bright light, they would fly into the mantles and break them. Mantles are incredibly delicate and fragile and, while there were numerous back-up mantles, insects like bluebottles could destroy them in no time.

The way the back-up system worked was very clever. Six mantles were arranged around in a clockwork gallery. A sturdy wooden peg about 25mm long and about 5mm in the square acted as a stop that the clockwork motor pushed against. If the mantle got broken it spilled a flame, which burned away the wood, and the gallery turned until it came to the next wooden peg and so a new mantle was installed.

The conversion to automation required skill and expertise and the main contractors, T L Arcus of Lerwick, were experienced in this work. They had a long and proud track record working for the Northern Lighthouse Board, not only in Shetland but throughout Scotland and in the Isle of Man.

A rather alarming incident occurred one day when work had to done on the dome. Out Skerries is quite a high tower, around 23 metres. One of the workers on the dome was a young man called Angus. He was nearing the end of an engineering apprenticeship. Angus was a skilful and popular member of the workforce. He came down to ground level and joined me in the radio hut, jumped up and perched on the bench. He was talking to me when, without warning, his voice trailed off and he fell off the bench and crashed, heavily, to the floor. He was wearing a safety helmet and this probably saved his head from injury. When I knelt down beside him he was in a dead faint. I made sure he was lying in such a way that he could breath freely and went to get help. By the time I got back he was beginning to come round but we all shuddered to think what could have happened if he had fainted while on the dome.

Up there he would wear a safety belt but that has to be released if the man has to move from one part of the dome to another. Angus protested that he was all right but there was no question of allowing him back on the dome. Instead he was sent ashore to get a medical check-up. In the event nothing was ever found wrong with him and he was soon back at work.

Thankfully it never happened again and the reason for his faint remained unknown. Jimmy Sandison, the boss, kept Angus working at ground level for the time being. In fact I am not sure that Angus was ever back on the dome again.

The most pleasing thing that happened during my first two weeks in Skerries was another phone call from Mr Dickson.

"Remind me," he said. "When is it that you want to get married?"

I told him that the date we had set was 5th October.

"How much leave you want?"

"As much as I can get," I rather timidly replied.

"Is four weeks any good to you?'

I replied that a month was brilliant. I expected two weeks at most. Indeed I would have settled for one week. The fact was that this stage of my lighthouse career was idyllic. I was working two weeks on and two off. The four weeks I had been allocated as wedding leave consisted of two lots of time off back to back with Jim Hardie filling the breach. I readily agreed to pay Jim back by working a month to allow him an equal amount of time off. My first two weeks in Skerries flew past and I made the journey, in the opposite direction, on the *Earl of Zetland*. I disembarked in Mid Yell and went home in the mail car.

Needless to say I was impatient to get to Gloup to see Margaret. My time home went by even faster than the time in Skerries. It was high summer, with regattas and other summer events in full swing and we had great fun. I well remember us coming home to Margaret's house in the early hours of the morning to find her brother John and a friend, home on holiday, boiling liver heads and young tatties. A great feed was had by all.

Everything was now in place for our big day in October. Of course much had to be done but now that I had the guarantee of leave all else seemed to fall into place. Margaret was going to be home all the time so she was well able to make the final arrangements and deal with things as they developed.

All too soon I was on my way to Lerwick again to stay overnight and catch the *Earl* on the Monday morning. The morning dawned dark and stormy but I was onboard in good time. It came as no great surprise when I was told the same story as the first time, namely that they would make up their minds about Skerries when they got there.

I was told, as before, that they would bypass Skerries and this before we were out of the harbour. Back I came to Mid Yell and was home overnight before arriving in Skerries a day late. I came in for some ribbing about this but folk in Skerries were all well aware of the tricks that the weather, and the *Earl*, could play.

The second two weeks in Skerries were, more or less, a repeat of the first. However the weather was not good. There was fog, wind and rain. One morning, when I arrived at the boat to go off to the lighthouse, Bobby Johnson asked if I had oilskins. I did not own such a thing and told him so. This was not good enough, he said. Without waterproofs I was going to get soaked on a regular basis and, in his view, I should have been issued with oilskins as part of my uniform. At night, when he took us ashore, he told me he had phoned HQ and they had agreed that I needed waterproofs. Not only that, but they would pay for them. I was, therefore, authorised to go to George William's shop and buy a suit. This I did that very day. I got a suit of green Helly Hansens that were high quality and quite easy to take on and off. Of course waterproofs were not needed every day and whether to carry them or not was a matter of judgment.

One doubtful morning I took the oilskins with me and was rewarded with approving looks. Andrew Anderson by contrast had left his at home and Bobby Johnson lost no time in telling him he had made a mistake. Andrew sought to justify his decision by saying that he believed it was going to be dry.

"Not the point," said Bobby. "We hae ta go ta Muckla Skerry."

Archie Williamson took up the story and in his slow, rather methodical way explained that the light on Muckla Skerry was not working. Archie was paid a small amount to monitor and log the minor light on the skerry. Andrew was loth to admit that he needed oilskins and therefore reluctant to agree that there was any need to go there.

Looking directly at Archie he demanded: "Is do sure it da light is oot?"

So astonished was Archie at such a question that he opened and shut his mouth several times before the power of speech returned to him.

"Androo, dus do tink it I wid phone Edinborro apu da middle o da nite if I wusna sure?"

Bobby, as well as all the rest of us, burst out laughing. It was yet another moment to treasure.

In the event I was put to the lighthouse, rather to my disappointment, and never made the trip to Muckla Sherry, which lies between Out Skerries and the Shetland mainland.

Living with the Williamsons was very enjoyable. Every evening Arthur and I sat in the kitchen and drank coffee while the others were in the sitting room watching TV. It was at those times that I heard a great many stories from him, stories about the fishing, some funny, some sad, but all worth hearing.

Arthur would bring out the big coffee mugs of the type often found on fishing boats, the ones that held a pint and were white with blue hoops on them. He would make strong, sweet coffee and the two of us sat at the table indulging in that great Shetland pastime, yarning.

He told me about one summer when the herring fishing was very poor. They were catching next to nothing. Nor were they alone in their lack of success. All the other boats were faring badly too. To compensate they set extra nets in an attempt to maximise their chances of a decent catch. One night they set the nets away to the east of Gulberwick with little expectation of success. To their surprise and delight, when they came to haul the nets, they were all full of prime herring. Such was the size of the catch that the hold was full to the brim with half the nets still in the water. To abandon the remaining nets was unthinkable, given that their season so far had been so poor. Another herring boat in the area responded to their signal and came alongside. It seemed that Arthur's boat had located the only shoal of herring because this boat had caught little or nothing. They were invited to haul the remaining nets. This they did, but they could not manage all the catch either and there were still nets, and herring, in the sea. The skipper then made an outrageous decision. He ordered the bulkhead, between the hold and the forecastle, to be breached. This meant that the herring filled the forecastle, covered the cooking stove, filled the crew's bunks and completely ruined everything eatable onboard. It was dangerous too in terms of safety. So heavily laden were they that they had no freeboard at all. The weather was good and the market, in Lerwick, was not so far away. They landed more herring that day than most of the other boats put together but they now had the job of trying to clean up. I asked Arthur if they were able to sleep in the bunks that day.

"Yea," he said. "Bit dey smelled o herring an dey wir kindo damp."

Arthur's sons took great delight in telling stories about their father and poking fun at him in a kindly and harmless way. Arthur could never be called a snappy dresser. Whatever he was going to wear he put on the way it came to him. Magnie said, one night, that when they were at the fishing with little or no sleep it was easy to lose track of the days of the week but their father's jumper kept them right. He said that on Mondays,

Wednesdays and Fridays it was on right side out but on Tuesdays, Thursdays and Saturdays it was outside in.

Fish formed an important part of the diet in Seaside Cottage. I love fish and we had some memorable feeds. Magnie used to bring home big cod heads. They came from huge fish that had been processed in the factory; some of those heads were bigger than a sheep's head. Magnie, Arthur and myself had them for supper and eaten with home-baked hufsey and butter it was a feed fit to set in front of a king. Very often Arthur, before he went off fishing, would ask me what sort of a fish I would like for my dinner. At first I thought that he was joking, so I said, at random, a ling. The following evening, when we sat down to eat, Arthur had a big grin on his face and, sure enough, a ling it was, and delicious. After that it became a joke of a different kind; no matter what I asked for it usually appeared on the table. It was a combination of someone with generations of knowledge and experience and the proximity of rich fishing grounds.

Another period of home leave came and went. As I was to discover in the years to come shore leave, time at home spent with loved ones, always passed quickly. No matter how pleasant the working time was it always took longer. This time around I travelled with the *Earl* and there was no problem with weather.

However, there was a big surprise waiting for me in Skerries. There was no work going on at the lighthouse because the contractor's men were off on their annual holidays. Nonetheless Donnie and I had to go through the motions and spend the same amount of time on the Bound Skerry. There was no work that we could do by ourselves. When the workmen were there they usually found something for us to do. There is an old saying that the devil always finds work for idle hands. Donnie could never be inactive, it was not in his nature, so we

embarked on the hardest, the most unnecessary and pointless work that any of us had ever done that, or any other, summer. We began to quarry rocks, and for no other reason than the sense of achievement at being able to move an object weighing tons with nothing more than levers. The end result was a huge splash and a nasty moment for the shags fishing under the cliffs.

Some days, if Donnie was busy doing something else I spent the days at the lighthouse by myself. I fixed a secluded area among the rocks, out of the wind, where I could sunbathe. Sometimes I dozed and even slept in my lair. The whole fortnight went past and the workmen did not return until I had gone home again on leave.

All during this period Margaret and I were saying to each other that the next time I came home it was our wedding, the event that we looked forward to above all else. We did everything it was possible to do in advance. Final preparations had to wait until nearer the time.

At the end of my leave I travelled to Lerwick on the Sunday night as usual. Walking along Commercial Street I was surprised to meet Arthur Williamson looking somewhat troubled. He said he was glad we had met up. He wanted to tell me that no-one was at home in Seaside Cottage because Stewart had had an accident and was in hospital.

Stewart had been injured at work. A heavy steel girder that was about to be placed in the new pier had fallen on his foot and badly injured his toes to the point that he was in danger of losing some of them. Stewart's mother was staying in Lerwick to be with him. Arthur had promised to do some trips with the

Bound Skerry.

Swiftwing so he told me I was to go to the house of his sister, Mary. She had promised to look after me until things returned to normal in Seaside Cottage.

This I did and found Mary to be as kind and welcoming as everyone else in Skerries. I saw no more of Arthur or Magnie until Tuesday night when they both came to Mary's house to tell us news of Stewart. He had needed an operation on his toes and this had been carried out. He had a recovery period to go through but it was, thankfully, all right in the end.

That same day Arthur had been in Vidlin but came home in the early evening just before Magnie finished work. Knowing that they were both going to be away they had made a big pot of tattie soup the previous evening that needed nothing more than reheating. A two-burner gas hob stood on the worktop near the window and as soon as he came in Arthur lit the ring under the pot and went straight to the phone to find out about Stewart's operation. When he came back the kitchen was so full of smoke that he could see nothing. He knew the soup had never had time to heat let alone burn and was completely at a loss to know what had happened.

Magnie then took up the story. "Whin I kam in I coodna see Daddy," he said. "I only kent it he wus dere whin he spak."

The source of the smoke was a mystery to the pair of them but they opened the door and the windows and allowed the smoke to clear. After a moment they saw what had happened. In lighting the gas Arthur had set fire to the curtains, which were thin and made from a flammable material. The curtains had burned away entirely leaving nothing but a short length of string that had held them up.

Donnie Henderson lights up for the last time.

In normal times events on the Scottish mainland are of little concern to Shetlanders but now something was happening that set alarm bells ringing. There was a dockers' strike and this meant that cargo might not get in or out of the islands. To confirm my worst fears Margaret rang to tell me she had been speaking to the local shopkeeper, Davy Thomason, and he had warned her that if the strike went ahead and if he could get no supplies to the shop then he would not be able to fulfil our order for drink for the wedding. We had placed a large order for booze. At a Shetland wedding in those days there was no bar and the wedding company supplied all the drinks for both nights. The way we saw it was that while we might overcome other shortages, no way could we have a wedding without alcohol.

Because of this we had to face the possibility that we might have to postpone the wedding. For all sorts of reasons this was heartbreak. All arrangements had been made and the invitations to over two hundred folk were out and my leave time would be wasted. We could do no more than keep our fingers crossed and hope that the strike would be called off.

For Magnie it was far simpler. When the news of the possible strike was broadcast on the radio he rose from the table and went out the door without finishing his tea. We all looked at each other but no-one knew where he had gone although clearly he was a man on a mission. After twenty minutes or so he reappeared, huffing and puffing, and heavy laden.

"Dey can strike noo as much is dey lik," he said and put a seventy-pound bag of oatmeal down on the floor.

Oatcakes and black treacle was his favourite food so he figured that if he got half a boll of meal from the shop while the going was good he would see out the strike in good order.

CHAPTER 24

THE WEDDING

TO OUR profound relief the strike was called off. Some sort of settlement had been reached; we little cared what. It was all systems go for the big day. We had a huge amount of support from our friends and families. In those days a traditional wedding was impossible without the help of the whole community.

Margaret's brother John was best man. He and Angus, Margaret's other brother, kicked off by rounding up and slaughtering seven hogs for the wedding feast. When those animals had been butchered the meat was distributed to helpers to be cooked and taken to the hall on the night. Also distributed were bags of flour to be baked into bannocks and fancies. Women were asked to "take a table". In the hall long trestle tables were erected and divided into units of twelve place settings. The women took their best china to provide the dishes and cutlery for a table of twelve. If anyone did not have a big enough tea set for twelve then a table would be divided again into a half table. They would also bring a cake stand, plates for bread and meat, teapot, sugar basin, butter dish and a cruet set.

The setting of the tables would take place a couple of nights before the wedding. It was the usual thing to cover the rough wooden surfaces with wallpaper turned upside down. The division between each woman's space was marked with a distinct lack of subtlety, a three-foot rule measured equal shares and a line drawn by a blue crayon marked the boundaries. This was before the availability of banquet roll. Margaret did not like the wallpaper much so she bought paper tablecloths. They did not meet with universal approval from the traditionalists because they inhibited the reckless use of the blue crayon.

The Cullivoe hall had no bar and, therefore, no glasses so, as others had done before, we hired glasses from a shop in Lerwick; half-pint glasses for beer, cider and soft drinks and smaller glasses for spirits. According to the old saying, there is many a slip twixt cup and lip and so it proved with our glasses. One of the boxes was dropped between the side of the *Earl* and the Cullivoe pier. The box fell into the sea to become soggy and useless and some of the glasses got broken. There was no insurance so breakages had to be paid for, that was part of the deal.

Another important part of the preparations was the decorations. Strings of bunting were stretched in the hall and outside. There was a net full of balloons to be released at some point during the night but the centrepiece was the back of the stage. Main man at this was my great friend Gordon Jamieson who was not only artistic but had an eye for detail and a determination to make everything as good as it could be. The end result was brilliant. Gordon constructed a lighthouse from crepe paper and put our initials in the beam of the light. The overall shape was based on a lighthouse keeper's cap badge, an oval. For anyone unfamiliar with lighthouses it was quite simply a highly attractive decoration but for anyone who knew about lighthouses it was a stunning creation that was truly memorable.

At last all the preparations were in place. There was scarcely a household or individual not involved in some way. The minister, the Rev Jim Blaikie, came to see us and we went to the kirk one afternoon to rehearse the wedding service. With us were John, the best man and Elizabeth, the bridesmaid.

The night before the wedding we were all at the hall again. All the refreshments had been delivered and the bar set up. This was in the clubroom of the hall, which opened off the kitchen while another door gave access to the stage. Davy Nisbet and Robert Anderson were in charge here. A short trestle table was set up to be the actual bar and behind it was the drink.

The barrels of beer and lager were made ready for use and all the beer jugs were washed and left in a handy place. Of course, when all the work was done everyone was given a dram, indeed as many drams as anyone wanted. For my part I made my excuses and went off to have an early night. I was determined to be on top form for the biggest day of my life.

It was back to the hall in the morning because it was then that the women were making the sandwiches. There was meat to slice and food to collect from the shops and from the bus. Some of the wedding company looked a little the worse for wear; the night before had strayed into the present day. It was the classic case of too many refreshments and too little shut-eye.

By lunchtime all was done and it was a case of spending a quiet afternoon waiting for the time to go to the kirk for real. As it turned out we had an unexpected visitor in the early afternoon, a total stranger. He was a tourist, a backpacker, probably a student. He was tired and hungry but I had other things on my mind and took scant interest in him. My mother invited him into the kitchen and gave him tea and sandwiches. He told us that his name was Richard Myles. He offered to pay for the food but my mother would have none of it. He was truly thankful for the hospitality and left a one pound note as a wedding present.

The backpacker was soon forgotten and it never occurred to me that some day I might see him again. See him again we did, some fifteen years later. After I left the lighthouse service Margaret and I started a café. We applied to the Highlands and Islands Development Board for a grant to buy kitchen equipment and who do think we had to apply to? Richard Myles.

I had a new suit to wear for the wedding. My father also bought a new suit and my mother had splashed out too. A fleet of cars arrived to take us to the kirk and what happened there is all a bit of a blur. I do remember that the bride arrived sooner than we expected. In my hurry I knocked over a heater in the vestry and the involuntary expletive that I uttered brought a sharp glance from Mr Blaikie.

The hall looked beautiful for the reception. We had deliberately restrained ourselves in the number of invitations we sent out. We had all seen weddings where the guests were packed together like sardines and we wanted our guests to be comfortable. And so it proved. The hall was nicely filled without being overcrowded. Dennis Coutts, the professional photographer from Lerwick, was on hand to capture the scene. Among the guests that I was delighted to see was Eddie Black and his lovely wife Georgie from Sumburgh Head. Equally

Wedding night in the Cullivoe Hall, 4th October, 1972. Photo by Dennis Coutts

176

welcome was the principal from Muckle Flugga, Alec Scott Tulloch and his wife Chris. Alec was another good friend; he regarded me as his protégé. Also present were Alex and Sheila Webster. Alex was the chief coastguard in Lerwick and they had been invited because Margaret's family had long been associated with the coastguards as auxiliaries.

Another guest who had come from a distance was Peter Cooke from the School of Scottish Studies in Edinburgh. Peter had been a frequent visitor to North Yell collecting the unique fiddle music of the Cullivoe Fiddlers. As always he was armed with his tape recorder and recorded the entire event, including the speeches.

The tables were laden with food and drink, the centrepiece being the mutton and bannocks that the whole community had helped to provide and prepare. There were lots of cakes, fancies and biscuits as well as tea. The young men of the place acted as waiters and the whole operation ran like a well-oiled machine. As time went on some of the component parts did, indeed, get well oiled.

When everyone had eaten their fill the wedding cake, the cutting of which kicked off proceedings, was taken into the hall on trays and passed up the long tables so that everyone got a piece. Some liked lots of icing while others wanted plainer pieces. All the glasses were refilled and the best man invited Davy Johnston to propose the toast to the bride. Davy was a family friend and a relative of Margaret's. He was also councillor for North Yell and Fetlar. He did his usual very able job and highlighted the fact that Margaret and I were both connected with life-saving services. Margaret's father and brothers were all coastguards and I was a lightkeeper.

I did the usual "on behalf of my wife and myself" bit that raised the usual raucous cheer and Dr Dawson Clubb proposed the toast to the bridesmaid to which John, the best man, replied. He then asked everyone to remain seated while the tables were cleared which, as always, was the signal for everyone to get to their feet and leave. The dishes, the best china that the women had brought, had to be packed into cardboard boxes or baskets, unwashed, to be dealt with the following day. Disasters were not unknown. Sometimes inebriated men tried to carry the baskets home only to trip and fall, doing untold damage to the precious contents. After the wedding feast the hall was cleared and the dancing began. Often the first dance was the bride's reel but not being much of a dancer I was not up to that so a grand march was followed by a Boston two-step. The music was provided by Gordon Jamieson and his Band that consisted of himself, his wife Anne on piano and his brother Victor on bass. It was still the practice for musicians to get fiddlers' bids; that is to say someone might be invited to a wedding because they were a musician rather than for any other reason. In our case Gordon had promised to play for the wedding so we had no worries on that score. The band was, by common consent, the best in Shetland to dance to.

Drinks provided by the wedding company were offered at regular intervals, after every third dance. Seats would be set down and a team led by the bride and groom would pass trays with glasses of whisky, rum, vodka, sherry and cider as well as soft drinks. Empty glasses were distributed ready to be filled from big jugs containing beer and lager. Junior members of the bridal party offered sweets. Early on Margaret and I left the hall for a period because we had some visiting to do. Some of our close relatives and friends could not be at our wedding, one who was bereaved and others who were unwell. When we got back Margaret performed another traditional bridal duty. She gave out favours to the nearest and dearest female guests.

A stop to the dancing was called at midnight, suppertime was declared and the seats set down once more. Cups were given out for tea and the wedding company served sandwiches, cakes and biscuits. Refills were offered and when all was collected and taken back to the kitchen the dancing resumed.

A wedding like ours required a lot of hard work by a great many folk. Without willing helpers it could never happen. Over many decades a system, a way of working, evolved. Key to its success was leadership. The clear duty of the best man and bridesmaid was to look after the needs and interests of the bride and groom. Even more important was the married man and married wife. They were responsible for the wellbeing of the guests and organised the hospitality, the passing of drinks and the like. The married folk were, as the term implies, older folk who were themselves married. The married man would come from the groom's side and the married wife from the bride's. Our team was Charlie Tulloch, my cousin, an excellent choice who was, as well as everything else, a great dancer, one of the very best in the hall. Adaline, sister of Gordon Jamieson, was the married wife. She was hugely experienced and expert in the way she carried out her duties.

There was no fixed time for the dance to come to an end. It was, quite literally, played by ear. After supper a lot of the older guests went home but that still left plenty to continue the dance. However at around three-thirty the company was beginning to flag and the last dance was announced. It was a prolonged Boston two-step that got everyone on the floor, and then there was a joining of hands for *Auld Lang Syne* and *For*

She's a Jolly Good Fellow. Margaret and I were both carried shoulder high around the hall to be united, still up in the air, with a kiss.

All this left two more things to do before we left the hall. Firstly I announced that the clearing up of the hall would be at 2pm and that the second night would start at 9pm. The last thing to do was for Margaret and I to go to the door and say goodnight to everyone and offer one last drink, for the road. We had to be the last ones to leave.

To get safely away from the hall caused me no little concern. It was the usual practice for some of the young blades to try and 'kidnap' a newly married couple and what they sometimes did to them did not bear thinking about. James Mann, Elizabeth's fiancé, offered to follow us and stop on a stretch of narrow road, thus causing a roadblock. This was all very well but it took no account of anyone who might be laying an ambush. As it was we were grabbed and bundled into a car and driven away before we had time to debate the matter any further and before we knew who our abductors were. In the event we were lucky, the two were Victor Jamieson and his cousin Robert. To capture a bride and groom was a mighty coup for them as teenagers and they had no thoughts of blackening us or giving us a tough time.

For our wedding night we had booked a room in a guesthouse, Sellafirth House. I was relieved when the boys dropped us off and there was no sign of any other mischief-makers. Nonetheless it was a magic moment when I able to lock the bedroom room, lock out the wedding guests and the whole world.

The following morning a taste of reality returned when my father came and picked us up in his somewhat disreputable three-wheeled Reliant Robin. Our house in Gutcher was full of people who had gathered for one reason or another. My mother, as usual, was making tea and to offer a dram seemed to be the civilised thing to do. We had a great morning of jokes, stories and good conversation but after dinner we all had to go and clear the hall and make ready for the second night. All the glasses had to be washed and dried. More meat had to be sliced and made into yet more sandwiches. The floor of the main hall had to be swept and scrubbed.

In the clubroom Davy and Robert were checking the stock of drink and making ready that side of things. Many hands make light work, they say, and soon it was all done and time to call on the barmen to dispense refreshments to keep us all going until the fun began again.

After tea we were able to have a short rest but we got dressed up and, of course, we had to be the first ones at the hall to greet the guests and give them a welcoming dram. On the first night of a wedding the numbers have to match the available seating but on the second no such restriction applies so the company is usually much bigger.

Gordon, Anne and Victor began to play again and the dance started with renewed gusto. It was the same procedure as the first night with seats brought in and drinks passed every third dance. Again supper was around midnight and everyone had a great time for Margaret and myself were far more relaxed. A second night is entirely informal. Dancing, eating and drinking went on even longer but eventually we had all had enough and it was time to call a halt. We had no gauntlet to run this time. We were unmolested and allowed to go to bed in peace.

The next day the hall had to be put to rights again and there were a great many loose ends to tie up. We had to return everything that had been borrowed and pack up the glasses that were going back to Lerwick, taking careful note of the number of breakages. There were many bills to pay, some to the local shop and others where the money had to be posted.

A wedding where several hundred guests are fed and given free drink for two long nights can be costly and ours was no exception. Our parents gave us generous gifts but money to pay for the wedding was our own responsibility. Before I became a lightkeeper I had no money at all and Margaret, as a student, was in the same boat. One factor that helped greatly was the practice of many to give money as a wedding present rather than household objects like toasters and electric kettles. In our case we received more money than the wedding cost. We were left with all the other presents that we valued greatly. To thank everyone for their presents was yet another thing to be done. When family and friends are so good as to give gifts to say thanks is the least you can do. When an announcement of the wedding was sent to *The Shetland Times* we decided that all was done and we could really begin our married life together.

We did not have the funds to have a honeymoon in some exotic location abroad in the sun so we settled for a week in Edinburgh. Our friend Peter Cooke travelled to Edinburgh with us and suggested a hotel that might be comfortable and within our means. So it proved. We enjoyed our stay in the Drummond and spent our days visiting friends and going around the city.

On our return we had the dilemma of deciding where we were going to stay. In truth I had never given this any thought but although we spent time with both sets of parents we settled in Gloup beside Margaret's folk, who embraced me as their son and as one of the family.

CHAPTER 25

THE LAST LAP

THE month's leave I had been given was soon over but looking back we had got a lot of mileage from it – wedding, honeymoon and all. To have to say goodbye to Margaret was harder now than it had ever been but we both realised that this was the way of our lives and our separation was temporary.

Nothing had changed in Skerries except that the conversion of the lighthouse to permanent automation was a stage nearer completion. We were given a date when it was to be finished, 12th December. The job ongoing when I returned was inside the lightroom near the top of the tower. It was to be lined with Formica sheets. These were eight foot by four foot sheets with a smooth, glass-like finish. They had to be stuck up with glue and the receiving surface had to be smooth and free from any grease, dirt or lumps. The glue was cellulose and had a powerful, intoxicating smell. It was vitally important to have good ventilation when working with it.

The adhesive came in big drums and was spread on to the sheets with small, toothed spreaders that left the surface of the glue ribbed. It was left until it was dry to the touch and then the sheet was put into place. Here great care had to be taken because the glue took a strong grip and if it went squint it was very difficult to take off again. When working with the glue it was impossible to keeps hands clean. We were not issued with any gloves. We worked with our bare hands and by stopping time our hands were caked with the stuff. Donny liked this. He said he enjoyed picking it off his hands; it gave him something to do in the evenings.

I continued to enjoy my stay with the Williamsons in Seaside Cottage. As time went on I became more and more one of the family. A weekly ritual took place in the family every Friday. Friday was papers day. Skerries folk, like Yell folk, set no value on daily papers but *The Shetland Times* was welcomed each week.

The Williamson household got a lot of papers and magazines and anyone bringing them from the shop would throw down a huge pile on the kitchen table. Arthur had no interest in any paper other than *The Shetland Times* and he was, without fail, the victim of a rather unkind prank. On the way home anyone who had the papers would extract the *Times* from the bundle and hide it under their jacket. Arthur had rather poor eyesight but he would go through the bundle time after time looking for *The Shetland Times*. In the meantime everyone else had had a look at it but he never saw or tumbled to what was going on. In the end someone would take pity on him and give him the paper.

Another home leave came and at the end of it Margaret and I decided to have the weekend in Lerwick. We went to Lerwick on the Friday and booked into the Queen's Hotel, spending a very pleasant three days. Margaret is not very happy in boats or ships but she agreed to travel with me on the *Earl* on Monday morning.

Monday morning turned out to be nasty weatherwise. Again I was never told, before we sailed, whether we were going to Skerries. As before the news came within minutes of leaving the pier that we were going to bypass Skerries so we went ashore in Mid Yell. To be put ashore anywhere that day was a relief. It was by far and away the worst day I had on the *Earl*. Judging by the sounds coming from the galley they had very few dishes left whole. The pitching and rolling was fierce and Margaret hated it. As before, I rejoined the *Earl* the following morning.

This spell of duty was to be my last in Skerries. However, this time it was to be longer because I had been given four weeks off instead of two at the wedding time and I had to pay that back. In any case, they needed every man they could muster to clear up everything and have it ready to ship out on the lighthouse ship *Pharos* on 12th December.

The shore station for the lighthouse was on the island of Gruney. It is the third biggest of the group of islands that makes up Skerries but is uninhabited. However, the lighthouse still retained a store there. One morning Donnie, two of the contractors' men and myself were sent to Gruney to clear out the store. We were told to pack everything that was useful into cargo nets to be shipped and burn or dump the rest. Bobby Johnson and his crew landed us there and we were to be picked up again in an hour or so. The store was small and we had the job done in next to no time. We sat or wandered around the island waiting for the boat to come back but they never did. We had all left our lunch boxes at the lighthouse because we believed we would be back in good time. We had no means of communication and as the afternoon wore on it became clear that Bobby had forgotten all about us. To be without food or water for a few hours did us no harm but we were all cold and hungry when night came. It was only when then the rest of the men were taken ashore that our plight was discovered and the boat came for us as something of an afterthought.

The *Pharos* arrived on the 11th because it was decided that there was too much to load and it could never be done in one day. The weather was pretty good given that it was mid-December and we worked all day assembling everything ready for shipment. A big shock awaited us on the morning of the 12th.

The boatswain of the *Pharos* announced that the ship's crew were working to rule and were not handling any cargo. That was, according to them, work for dockers and under no circumstances would they do it. The NLB and the contractors were counting on the help of the seamen. Much of the cargo was too heavy to be lifted with the hands available.

Rather like a football captain winning the toss of the coin and deciding to play with the wind we began by shipping the items we could handle and leaving the more difficult things for the time being. I think the hope was that the seamen might come around and work normally. In the event they sat in the boat. They never set foot on shore, but as soon as they had a load they set off to the *Pharos* with it, came back and the same procedure followed. To try and help matters along the ship's chief engineer and Captain Fraser came on to the Bound Skerry to help us.

Captain Fraser proved to be a senior officer who was due to retire sooner rather than later. He was a small lean man who, willing to help as he was, had little in the way of brute strength. He was from Aith originally and seemed more interested in discussing the hill dykes with Jimmy Sandison, the contractor's foreman, than he was in the seamen and their industrial action. Jimmy was from Aith too.

I found him trying, in vain, to up-end a fifty-gallon barrel of petrol. I ran to help him but, unfortunately, I knocked off his white hat. It fell on the filthy ground and when the barrel came over the point of balance the legging came down on top of it so that half of it was under the barrel.

On the Bound Skerry the lighthouse is built on the highest point. For cargo purposes a short length of track had been laid down to the landing place. The slope was steep enough that a bogey would run down by means of gravity while a winch powered by a diesel engine hauled it back up again. This rail link was the means by which we took items of cargo from the lighthouse to the ship's boat. Our big problem was lifting the heaviest of it into the bogey. All things considered we got on well but I could not see, for the life of me, how we were going to manage to take the engine to the boat. The engine and the winch were mounted on a cast iron bed that was bolted to a concrete base and must have weighed well over a ton. John Robson, the artificer, was in charge of clearing the station. When I asked the question it was clear that this problem was giving him a headache.

"I'm thinking, I'm thinking," was all he said.

By mid-afternoon almost everything else was shipped and we were all tired. It had been a back-breaking day made worse by the fact that we had to endure not only the seamen's inactivity but their taunts and jeers when anything went wrong. It was difficult not to answer back or threaten violence.

Daylight was fading fast when John said he had figured out how to get the engine, the winch and the bed to the boat. He told me to get Donnie and the three of us would do it. He did not want anyone on the job who was not employed by the lighthouse board in case it all went badly wrong. He ordered Donnie to take the steel cable which hauled the bogey and stretch it all the way down to the landing and make it securely fast. He gave me a spanner and told me to remove the nuts from the bed bolts. We used crowbars to lever the bed complete with engine and winch off the concrete base.

It was only then that the hare-brained plan he had hatched dawned on me. He was going to start the engine, put the winch in gear and it would, with a huge slice of luck, haul itself to the landing area. There was nothing to keep it within the rails. It was top heavy and to go near it was dangerous and foolhardy. What was abundantly clear was that if it were left to itself it would topple over and never see the *Pharos* either that day or any day in the near future. Undaunted, John perched himself on top of this contraption while Donnie and I were stationed on either side with a length of wood each, four by two, the idea being that if it looked like falling over we jammed the wood in, as a prop, to keep it upright. The railway line was raised away above ground level so this steel colossus towered above us in a truly terrifying manner. John put it into gear but it moved about two feet only before it jammed in the rails, shuddered to a halt and Donny had to use his prop to avoid disaster. With crowbars we straightened it up again and gained another few feet before it got stuck and John had to knock it out of gear.

And so it went on. Several times when it rocked and swayed drunkenly I thought my number was up but miraculously we always managed to get the props in place in the nick of time. Progress was painfully slow but eventually we got to the landing with whole skin and bones.

I don't, to this day, know how long it took but, despite the December chill, I was soaked with sweat and had exhausted about a year's worth of adrenalin. Even now we still had to get it into the boat. The seamen were all sitting watching, smoking, eating biscuits, mocking our efforts and telling us that if we did not hurry up they would go back to the ship without the engine.

John Robson had boards prepared which he lashed on to the boat and the pier to form a bridge and a skid. The boatswain was unhappy about the boards. He seemed to think they infringed his territory. He even threatened to remove them. John told the seamen, in no uncertain terms, that they were not to interfere with the boards. He told them that if they did they would be reported to the superintendent for sabotaging his work and causing danger to those of us who were working. He further warned that they were likely to face harsh disciplinary measures. We removed the engine and the winch from the bed to lighten it all.

The contractor's men could help now but even so we had to use crowbars and levers to lift the parts and rig ropes to restrain them. At last and to everyone's profound relief it was safely placed in the boat piece by piece and sent to the ship.

By this time it was pitch dark. We gathered all that was going to the shore together and loaded it into Bobby Johnson's boat. And so it was that I left the Bound Skerry for the last time. Of course it also meant that it was time to say goodbye to the Williamson family and all the friends I had made in Skerries and I went home the following day to a future I could not predict.

CHAPTER 26

APPOINTMENT

I PHONED HQ to report to Mr Dickson that I had finished in Skerries. He thanked me and said I would hear from him very soon but told me I was to be on leave until after Christmas and the New Year. This was great news. I had two weeks holidays and the festive season at home.

I found it strange to be home but not staying with my parents. Margaret and I stayed in Gloup with her family. The very next day there was a message from my mother. I was to phone Mr Dickson as soon as possible. My first thought was that some emergency had occurred and that my Christmas leave was cancelled but the news was a lot better than that.

Mr Dickson congratulated me and told me my appointment had come through. I had been appointed to Cape Wrath as second assistant. I was to proceed there as soon as possible after the New Year. Our effects were to be packed and I was to get quotes from two separate removal companies for the delivery to Durness in Sutherland.

As for ourselves, we were to book flights from Shetland to Wick. He gave me the phone number of MacKays in Durness. They ran taxis and had a hotel. I was to organise them to pick us up in Wick and to book us into the hotel for one night. The excitement of being appointed made it difficult for me to take all this in but I knew that I could contact Mr Dickson again if need be.

My first reaction to being appointed was one of delight. I had waited for this moment for over twenty months. Now all the travelling and hardships of life as a supernumerary were over. I was an established lightkeeper, a full member of this proud profession

A second and more sober look at the situation brought a tinge of disappointment. Cape Wrath was a station that no-one wanted; a station that, when they were there, everyone wanted away from. This negative thought was soon banished, especially when I discussed it with Margaret. Her thoughts were entirely positive. We were going to have our own home. It was a shore station and we were going to be together and, for her, that was enough to be going on with. Any problems would be dealt with as and when we encountered them. Cape Wrath had no fears for her and, therefore, none for me either.

I made all the arrangements as suggested by Mr Dickson. A company called Shore Porters were to do the removal. It was no huge job anyway. We had four tea chests full of wedding presents, our clothes and little else except a three-piece suite of furniture that we had chosen in Lerwick which was, in effect, a wedding present from my parents.

Now we could relax and enjoy Christmas and New Year and I never remember a festive season that I enjoyed more. It seemed to be an endless round of parties, music, visiting, eating and drinking. All my old friends were around. The company was wonderful.

CHAPTER 27

CAPE WRATH

ALL GOOD things come to an end and so it was with the holiday break. We had the prospect of our new life together and were quite keen to get to Cape Wrath and see our new home. Our effects had to be shipped to Aberdeen and from there Shore Porters took over.

As with everything else in those days our possessions had to be labelled and shipped out on the *Earl of Zetland*. My friend Gordon Jamieson came on the Friday morning with a minibus and we put it all to the store at the Cullivoe pier to wait for the next calling of the steamer.

We travelled to Wick on the Monday and were met by a stocky, robust-looking man who introduced himself as Richard MacKay. Already we knew the name Dickie MacKay and were slightly confused as to whether they were one and the same. Richard quickly put us right on that score. They were cousins, but very different in every way, as we were to learn.

We left Wick and headed towards Durness, a large scattered village that is the nearest habitation to Cape Wrath. On a standard map, such as we had at school, the north coast of Scotland looks something of a wilderness area with hardly any detail. I was looking forward to seeing the countryside but the end of the short winter day meant we saw little of the place. As we drove on Richard spoke about the places we were passing and wherever there was a pub he suggested a break for refreshments. I lost count of the number of stops we made but I have always remembered The Brass Tap in Tongue.

From Wick to Durness is very long drive but, despite all the stops, we got there eventually and Richard introduced us to Dickie and his wife Dottie, but not before he had warned us that his namesakes were strict teetotallers and ran a temperance hotel, not that it made any difference to us.

Dickie could tell us that our crates and furniture had arrived safely and were in the store. We got something to eat and spent a comfortable night there. In the morning after breakfast I phoned the station and spoke to the principal lightkeeper, Donald MacAuley. Through him arrangements were made for the boatman to take us and our belongings across the Kyle of Durness.

It was flat calm, there was not a breath of wind and it was very mild for the time of year. We stood and gazed across the water full of wonder while we waited for the boat. When it arrived, it was little bigger than a dinghy but for all that we had it could do the job in two trips.

The boatman was a small dark man, probably in his fifties. His name was Charlie Campbell and he and his wife lived at the pierhead on the other side, the Cape Wrath side. Donald MacAuley, who had the station tractor and trailer to carry the heavy stuff, met us. Also there was Brian Johnson, a Shetlander, who had a beat-up old car. Brian was a mechanic who had breathed life into this old banger because the station Land Rover was broken down, so there was nothing but the tractor to serve the station. It is eleven miles from the Kyle to the station, eleven miles of rough track suitable for a Land Rover or a tractor but little else.

Brian's old car struggled. The ridge of earth and grass in the middle of the road scraped the bottom of it all the way and Brian had to try and pick the smoothest path whenever that was possible. However, so narrow was the road that there was little choice. After about a mile we came to a river that had no bridge across it; it had to be forded. This was easy enough with a suitable vehicle, the water was only six or nine inches deep, but the car made heavy weather of it. It said a lot for the old car and for Brian's skilful driving that it was possible at all. Without misadventure we arrived at the station and were shown the home that we had looked forward so much to having.

It had no surprises. I had seen so many lighthouse dwellings that were exactly the same as the houses at the Cape. A quick look round revealed a small kitchen, living room, bathroom and three bedrooms. Mrs MacAulay and Mrs Johnson came to meet us and make us welcome. Mima MacAulay came from Skye. She and Donald, from Lewis, had a small son, eighteen-month-old Donald Angus. Brian's wife was Babs, from Fladdabister in Shetland. They too had a son, Billy, who was a year old. Mima had a meal waiting for us, which we greatly appreciated.

Donald told me I had the night off. I was to concentrate on getting settled in and anything we needed we were just to ask for. Even when our belongings were put in place in the house it was still a bit Spartan. As a young married couple there was much we did not have.

Lightkeepers' houses were partly furnished. We had a sideboard, wardrobes and beds and the floors were covered in Admiralty-type lino. In the kitchen we had a gas cooker, a sink, cupboards with pot and pans, cutlery and crockery and a paraffin fridge. However, all was not well with a number of things.

The previous incumbent had been a single man whose housekeeping skills left much to be desired. He had washed out the fridge with Jeyes Fluid and the smell of it met you in the face every time you opened the door. Margaret tried to wash it out and the neighbours suggested several solutions but nothing worked.

We washed it with vinegar and put cut onions in it and, on fine days, we carried it outside and left it, with the door open, in the wind. We thought we had cured it but when we put canned fruit in an airtight plastic container in the fridge overnight we found it to be seriously tainted. In the end we had to give up and do without a fridge.

The very same man who had been so diligent in washing out the fridge with such disastrous results had failed to sweep the chimney. It was all but blocked and when we lit coal in the grate the chimney took fire and the lum can split and fell on the roof. I had to wait until it all cooled off before replacing the chimney pot.

The plumbing gave us problems too. The pipes which brought water to the sink in the kitchen forever air-locked and to clear them was a daily task. The water, even when obtained, was unfit to drink. It was about the colour of brown ale and unfit for human consumption. It was no use even for cooking. For drinking water and cooking the only water we had was what was caught off the roofs. All the rones and gutters were piped into water tanks. Of course birds sat on the roofs and this water was unsafe unless it was first boiled. Electricity, too, was in short supply.

In many ways Cape Wrath was more like a rock station and

it eventually became one, with the families of lightkeepers living elsewhere.

The electricity supply came from generators housed in an engine room along with the compressors that drove the foghorn. The generators consisted of three Rushton-Hornsby units that, on paper, produced an output of 15kw. In practice they could never do this. The engines were old and inefficient. They smoked, leaked oil, and were difficult to start. They were run, one on load and the other two on standby. This meant that electricity had to be used sparingly. It was all right to have lights in the houses but little else and certainly no electric fires. The women would meet most mornings in a sort of St Kilda parliament to decide who was going to wash or iron or do anything else that would embarrass the generators.

Occasionally a generator would be heard to falter so the man on watch would have to go around switching off all non-essential usage. If the overloaded generator had overheated then another was started and a switchover effected. For this system to work at all families had to co-operate and get on well together otherwise there would be constant chaos.

For many women shopping is an important part of their routine. Here, however, no shopping in the usual manner was possible. The source of all the food and everyday items came from Dickie MacKay's shop in Durness but to go there in person, especially in the wintertime, was all but impossible.

With the Land Rover working it could be done but the usual way of shopping was to phone the shop on a Monday afternoon and give them a list of needs. They would then make it up into boxes to be taken across the Kyle on Wednesday whenever the tide was favourable. At the lighthouse we would be in touch with Charlie Campbell and he would tell us what time he would

make the crossing. The man whose watch began at 6pm would go to the ferry and collect the goods. Using the tractor and given the rough road, this took about two hours for the round trip. If you had forgotten anything there was not much help for it, you either had to borrow from the neighbours or do without until the next week. Every week, high on the list, was lemonade and bottled water because of the lack of drinkable water.

We arrived at Cape Wrath on 9th January 1973. It was an exciting time for us, a new year in every sense of the word to look forward to, but it was also an important time nationally. Edward Heath was Prime Minister and fulfilled a long-held ambition when Great Britain became, on New Year's Day, a full member of the European Common Market.

In terms of slotting into my job there were no problems. There was nothing at Cape Wrath that was entirely new to me. Nonetheless it was a complete station. It had a fog signal, a radio beacon and was a weather station.

The light was paraffin, a 55mm Stone Chance lamp of the type that was usual at most stations. There were two pieces of meteorological equipment I had not seen before. We had a hand-held anemometer to measure the wind speed and a crystal ball on the roof of the engine room to measure the hours of sunshine.

The anemometer was something of a damp squib; depending where you were on a windy day you could get almost any reading that you wanted. The idea was to take the reading in a place where the wind speed was not distorted by the cliffs, the buildings or the hills. On most occasions this was not easy.

Cape Wrath. © Northern Lighthouse Board.

Cape Wrath is the most north-westerly point of the Scottish mainland. Looking out from the top of the tower to the left was south; you were looking down the west coast. To the right was east looking along the north coast towards Strathy and Caithness beyond. The cliffs near the lighthouse are high. Behind our house they were some 420 feet but, as usual at lighthouses, a protective wall prevented anyone from falling over by accident. The fog signal was situated there too. When it was started up in the night it tended to put paid to any more sleep. It was surprising how quickly you got used to the sound of the horn. In fact you could waken up in the night, wonder why, and then realise that it was because the foghorn had been shut down.

The lighthouse station at Cape Wrath dates from 1828 and was the work of Robert Stevenson. It was the heyday of lighthouse building and at a time when it was still believed that to build on high headlands was a good idea. Like Sumburgh Head and many others the light was often obscured by fog or low cloud and, therefore, of little value to mariners.

Some eighty years later, before the First World War, Robert Stevenson's grandson made ambitious plans to relocate the lighthouse. It was to be on a skerry that lies a short distance offshore. He was going to link the new tower by two bridges to adjacent reefs and access from the shore was to be by a lift in a vertical shaft set back from the cliff edge. Work began on this project in June 1914 and the lift shaft was sunk to a depth of 50 feet. Work was stopped when there was a disagreement with the contractor, and with the outbreak of war the scheme was abandoned and never resumed. The shaft was still there but covered up by a heavy wooden lid.

There is no doubt that Cape Wrath is the most isolated place on the British mainland. The area between the lighthouse and the Kyle of Durness is a completely empty wilderness called the Parph that covers over 60,000 acres. It is the only place in the British Isles where warships are allowed live ammunition ashore and Garvie Island is a target for NATO's heaviest bombers to drop massive bombs on. We used to watch while all this happened. It was like being at a giant fireworks display. Every time before Garvie Island was to be bombed a big aircraft would fly low over the island to scare away the seabirds. Somewhat reluctantly they would fly off but as soon as the bombing stopped they would all come back again.

Having no Land Rover we were unable to leave the station. The only contact with the outside world was the weekly call to the shop and fetching the goods. For each lightkeeper it meant a trip to the ferry every three weeks while the women were never away at all.

It also meant that we did not always have occasional keepers to give us our days off. Early on in our spell at the Cape we had two occasional keepers, Bobby Morrison and Brian Kerr. Bobby was from Durness, a man up in years, quiet and totally dependable. Brian was very different from Bobby in attitude, something of a dropout, a hippie. He had a protest mentality that sought to challenge and contradict all governmental authority. Brian had a liking and admiration for any rebel wherever in the world they lived.

Over time Brian and I had many heated arguments while we worked together in the lighthouse but we started and finished each day as friends. Brian was born in South Africa and had an educated accent that completely contradicted his militant views. Brian and his wife, Maureen, had come to the north to be part of the Balnakeil craft village. There had been an RAF base there, part of the much-vaunted early warning system, but it proved to be useless and closed down. Rather than demolish the buildings the base had been offered, divided into units, as places where craft workers could ply their various trades. It turned out to be hard going for many of them and Brian had applied, and was accepted, as an occasional lightkeeper at Cape Wrath.

When occasional keepers were unavailable the regular lightkeepers had to continue working seven days a week and we could not get days off. This did not trouble us much because it meant we were hoarding days off so that when an occasional, or a supernumerary, came to relieve us we had enough holidays coming that we could go away for a short break.

At this time we got a new boatman. Charlie Campbell resigned and John Muir was appointed in his place. John came from Falkirk. His wife Cathy was born in Boat of Garten on Speyside. John proved to be very agreeable and well suited to the job. He was always ready and willing to take us across the Kyle.

On the face of it going to and fro across the voe looked like a very simple task without much seamanship or boat handling skills required, but there was more to it than met the eye. The Kyle would ebb dry but never so dry that you could wade from one side to the other. There was so much fresh water flowing that even with the lowest tide there were channels, like rivers, meandering through the sandbanks. However, that did not mean the boat could not be used. There was a real danger that the boat could get stuck, sand warped and might not float up when the tide came in. The boatman had to be able to judge the state of the tide and whether or not it was safe to go through the channels, working his way from one side to the other. Sometimes a landing had to be made that was nowhere near the pier. Whenever any cargo needed taking across, including the groceries from the shop, John would wait for high tide.

CHAPTER 28

LIFE AS AN ALK

BY THIS time we had settled in to the routine of the station. We were paid monthly, firstly by cheque, and later the money was paid directly into the bank. My salary was about £100 per month. This was enhanced by extra payments for doing the weather observations and works orders.

We also had a few perks that, in effect, added to our pay. We had free lighting and heating. Every family got three tons of coal delivered by the lighthouse ship as part of the annual stores. Lightkeepers were issued with uniforms and a points system was introduced so that individuals could decide what they needed. Each man was given something like 100 points and each item of uniform was given a value. For example, a greatcoat would be 70 or 80 points whereas a tie might only be a single point. We got uniform suits, made from quality material with double-breasted jackets with brass buttons with the lighthouse crest on them. We also got waterproof suits, welly boots, shoes, overalls, gloves, hats, white shirts and ties. There was no excuse for not being smart on inspection days or when travelling. Even at the most remote rock stations lightkeepers always wore uniform, a white shirt and tie, on relief days.

As winter gave way to spring life at the Cape changed and became easier. The Land Rover was eventually fixed and it was possible to leave the station and even go to Durness. Sometimes, especially on Wednesdays when the messages were fetched from the ferry, it was the practice to go across with the ferry and have a drink in the Cape Wrath Hotel. The staff at the hotel were always good to us folk from the lighthouse. The bar was never shut to us and it seemed that the kettle was always on the boil. Tea, coffee, sandwiches and biscuits were in plentiful supply. As we were in the hotel more often we got to know the locals, the folk who were regular customers.

Sometimes two lightkeepers and their wives would go together to the hotel for something of a night out. The hotel did not always adhere rigidly to the licensing hours. This suited the tourists, the lightkeepers and indeed the entire clientele. Even the local policeman took a rather indulgent view. In those days the bar was supposed to close at 10pm. If the policeman did not show up by that time then you could be certain that you would never see him at all. If he did put in an appearance he would always put his head around the door and say hello to everyone, this to give the barmaid fair warning that she should shut on time.

The bar had a warmth and friendliness about it that few other places can ever match. It was small. In the summer when the tourists were in large numbers it had a packed, claustrophobic atmosphere that made it feel like a pub in a small Irish town. In the winter when very few folk were there it still had a comfortable, relaxed air. The small tables dotted around all had wrought iron legs. The fact that most of them had the word 'Singer' worked into the decorations made it easy to deduce that they started life supporting sewing machines. The fate of the machines was another question altogether.

Trips to the hotel were something we all looked forward to. It eased the routine of daily life at the Cape. I was, of course, junior man and had a number of things I was responsible for. As a rule the junior man had most work to do. It was just the way that lighthouses were always run. I had to clean the vaporiser and in winter that was every day. I had done this as a Super many times before. I took the view that if I was cleaning the vaporiser then I was not doing anything else. Another of my duties was to keep the weather records. This took some considerable time and had to be done with great care.

Lightkeepers were paid extra for doing weather observations. It was not a lot of money but it all helped. Like the extra money we got for work authorised by works order it was paid quarterly and the PLK was responsible for keeping records of who had been involved. Sometimes occasional keepers were in for a few days at a time and supernumeraries had to be counted in as well.

Cape Wrath was a full weather station. We took weather observations every three hours and sent the details, by phone, to the Met Office at Wick Airport. Such observations played little part in weather forecasting but the records were filed and used in the study of climate and climate change. The daily log that recorded the observations was full of the codes that made the information easy to forward to the Met Office but it was not in plain language so it had to be transcribed into a book that could be read by anyone interested in its contents. Any lightkeeper doing this job usually worked at it during the 2am until 6am watch. It was a good time to do it because there was peace and quiet. All the books and some of the weather instruments were housed in the quarterdeck built around the base of the tower. There was also a desk and good lighting so it was a case of working at it during the night. In fact it helped to pass the time and the room at the base of the tower was a handy place to be when keeping a wandering watch.

Strictly speaking, the man on watch was supposed to be in the lightroom with the machine that drove the light. This was not practical at Cape Wrath and many other stations. The watchkeeper had to go to the engine room several times during the watch and the weather observations were done every three hours. In the case of Cape Wrath the engine room was about sixty yards away from the tower. Given the decrepit state of the generators, close attention had to be paid to them.

If fog came the siren had to be activated and this increased the need to visit the engine room. It was a strange irony that the lightroom in a lighthouse never had much light in it. It was situated underneath the lens and the thrust of the main light was to shine out, seawards, and not anywhere else.

Donald and Mima had a delightful dog called Brandy. He was big and rough, a bearded collie of sorts. He was friendly with everyone and liked nothing better than someone to throw a stick, a stone or anything for him to fetch back. Sometimes he swallowed stones and this resulted in him having an emergency visit to the vet. After that we were careful not to throw anything he could swallow. When Donald and Mima went on holiday he used to stay with us. The day they went away he would come into our house, lie on the rug and make himself at home. Whenever Donald and Mima returned he went back home and became their dog again.

One rather naughty thing he did was to seriously distort the rainfall readings. Precipitation was collected in a funnel at ground level. One day, when I was on watch, I got a phone call from the Met Office in Wick. They were none too pleased and were querying the weather report that I had phoned in. I had reported several millimetres of rain. I had measured it carefully as we always did. However, the man on duty in Wick pointed out that I had reported minimal cloud cover and they were clouds that were entirely inconsistent with precipitation of any kind. The final nail in the coffin of my report came when he pointed out that no-one else was reporting any rain at all.

I felt like a total idiot and began to wonder how such a thing had happened. I thought that perhaps the man on watch before me had failed to empty the rain gauge but when I looked back to the previous report he had sent in he had reported no rain so, therefore, the rain gauge had been dry. I told Donald and Brain what had happened but they were inclined to laugh. They were in no way concerned nor did they seem to look on it as being important. Not, that is, until the same thing happened to Brian and the whole thing was looked on in a totally different light. A day or two later the mystery was solved. As the three of us left the workshop I heard Donald laughing and then scolding. Brandy was standing with one hind leg cocked in the air peeing with unerring accuracy into the rain gauge.

Ever after that the rainfall measured at Cape Wrath was more approximate than true and how much the doings of that wayward canine distorted the study of climate will never be known. A more immediate difference was that lightkeepers washed their hands more often than before.

Brandy was almost like another lightkeeper. No matter what job was being done he was always there or thereabouts and he loved the days when we went to the landing place. There was a jetty and a store about a mile and a half from the lighthouse. It was here that all the annual stores were landed. Most of the stores and everything intended for the houses was taken to the station right away but other stores like barrels of derv, paraffin and petrol were fetched as and when we needed them. To put the barrels on the trailer was an all-hands job although we did have a ramp to make it easier.

Brandy would run behind the tractor but as he got tired he would take short cuts and after about three trips he was lagging behind. He never gave up and when we had our coffee break he would have a rest too.

One day Donald and I went to the landing to fetch a barrel of petrol. It was just the one barrel and the one trip so we used the Land Rover instead of the tractor. This was bad news for Brandy because the Land Rover, old and decrepit as it was, was much faster than the tractor and he was hard-pushed to keep up. He arrived at the landing behind us with his tongue hanging out and blowing hard. We loaded up the barrel and set off back to the station without giving him any thought. Halfway back there was a screeching noise, Donald was sure that it was a wheel about to seize up.

Of course he did not stop because his goal was to get the old Land Rover to break down beyond repair. He had long campaigned for a new one and had no intention of nursing it along. He told me to look out the window and tell him if I could see or smell any smoke. I could see nothing. The noise got worse and worse and it was difficult to tell where it was coming from. Donald eventually stopped but the noise continued and when I looked around I discovered Brandy. He knew that the pace was too hot for him so he had stowed away in the back. Unfortunately for him the barrel of petrol had rolled on top of him. He was being crushed and it was him that was making all the noise. We rolled the barrel away from him and he got out and was none the worse but, ever after that, he was a bit cautious about travelling in the back of the Land Rover.

Brandy was a remarkably faithful and obedient dog. Once Donald left him in the Land Rover at the ferry while he went across to Durness. He told Brandy to stay because intended to be there for a short time only but the wind got up suddenly and the boat was unable to cross the Kyle. As it turned out it was another four days before Donald was able to return. When he got across he found Brandy exactly where he had left him. It was not that he was locked in the Land Rover. It was that he waited, as he had been told, patiently until his master returned. The rest of us at the lighthouse suffered more than Brandy did because we had to double up and do extra watchkeeping.

The spring was very dry and our water supply, such as it was, dried up. The same thing had happened in the past because there were barrels in the store at the landing for such an eventuality. We loaded the barrels on to the trailer and went to the Kearvaig River to fill them up. We had a stirrup pump so it was a case of pumping each barrel until it was full and then taking them to the station to eke out the supply.

The heather was bone dry too and someone had set fire to it. The fire burned for weeks, sometimes quite brightly and at other times it would die down until one wondered if it had finally gone out. A windy night would bring it back to life and a deep glow would come from a huge peat brae that the last of the fire was in.

One day Margaret and I went to have a look at it and I did a very stupid thing. I climbed on to the top of the brae. It was warm, even hot in places. What I had not realised was that the fire had burned inside it and made it hollow. The crust collapsed beneath my weight and I fell into the fire below. Needless to say I tried to get out quick but the hole that I was in was about five feet deep and the edges were dry, crumbly and very brittle. In the end I was lucky. I managed to get out with nothing worse than a fright and scorched trousers. My walloping around among the fire caused it to flare up again and if I been in that hole for much longer it could have been very serious indeed.

As soon as weather allowed we began the outside work and the first job was lime washing. Lime wash is the most dazzling white that can ever be applied to a stone wall and yet, in its raw state, it is an ugly and evil material to work with. It looks for all the world like rubble, grey and lumpy. Every lighthouse had large galvanised tanks to slake the lime in. A tank would be half-filled with lime and filled with water. The introduction of water could be quite spectacular, it would bubble, froth and boil and every keeper treated it with the utmost respect. To get sparked with it was to get nasty burns, not only from the heat but also from the corrosive nature of the stuff. Lightkeepers were not, as a rule, timid creatures but wearing gloves and goggles was a sensible precaution.

At one station the keepers fell on the bright idea of spraying on the lime wash, with disastrous results. When trying to clear a blockage one lightkeeper got a jet of lime in the face and lost an eye. After that HQ issued stern warnings about the need to be careful when working with quick lime.

Lime washing the tower was a three-man job. All lighthouses had a stage suspended from the balcony rail by hooks that ran on rollers and it was hoisted and lowered by blocks and tackles. Men working at heights were always at risk so before anything else was done the stage and the ropes that suspended it were carefully examined to make sure they were fresh and safe. Any rope that was in the least bit suspect was renewed and, that done, work began on the rigging of the stage.

The hooks and tackles had to be carried up the stairs to the top of the tower and out on to the balcony. Each tackle was too heavy for one man to carry but when they were hooked on to the rail the other ends were dropped to the ground and made fast to the stage. The two keepers who were to work on the stage set in buckets of lime and brushes and hauled the stage up to the top and made the ropes fast below. Then came the bit I hated. We had to climb over the balcony rail and hang on by our hands and dangle above the stage. When we knew that we were directly above we had to let go and drop into the stage. That took every ounce of courage I possessed but I saw how Brian did it so I followed suit. We took the strain of the ropes and the man below, Donald, let go.

The ropes were made fast to a cleat and the brushwork began. The one good thing about lime wash was that it never took long to apply. As soon as the section was done the stage was lowered to the next comfortable level. The ropes were never taken off the cleat entirely. They were unwound and eased to allow the stage to descend and so on until the stage was so low that the work could be reached from the ground. There was always a break and someone would climb up the stairs again to the balcony and move the hooks along to the next position. The tower at Cape Wrath was not so tall and if things went well the job could be done in one day.

Numerous other buildings at the station were lime washed but they could all be done from ladders. After working on the stage for a time I felt the first knuckle on my right hand very sore. When I looked at it I was horrified by what I saw. In my nervous excitement working in what to me was a very uncomfortable environment I had lost a piece of skin. The lime had got into the raw fresh and it had burned until I could see the white of the bone. I got it bandaged but it was very painful and took a long time to heal. I suppose it was my own fault because I was not wearing gloves. I never feel comfortable with gloves but I never lime washed again with bare hands.

Everyone was relieved when the lime washing was finished. The painting of doors and windows was pleasant work by comparison, especially if the weather was warm. At the Cape there was quite a lot of grass to cut and in the middle of summer it grew very fast and had to be cut almost every week.

With summer came the tourists. A minibus driven by Hughie Morrison ran up and down from the ferry every day and in the course of a summer took hundreds of visitors to see the lighthouse and the Parph. It was the job of the man on watch to greet visitors. There was no rule that said that visitors had to be shown around but we always did it unless we were very busy otherwise.

Of course lightkeepers looked for tips from the visitors but it was strictly forbidden to ask for money or even hint at such a thing. Some keepers tried various ploys to get tips but they seldom worked. At one station an off-duty keeper, not in uniform, would mingle with the visitors. He would make sure he was the first one downstairs and make a big show of giving the on-duty man a handsome tip. It was designed to set an example.

At another station a keeper, showing visitors around, placed a small brass tray on the table at the bottom of the tower with three half crowns in it, half crowns being the highest value coins at the time. When he went to check the tray with a view to gathering in the takings he found to his utmost dismay that not only had he got no tips but his three half crowns had disappeared.

Many visitors had never seen a lighthouse before and even fewer understood the foghorn. One foggy day when I was on duty the horn was blowing mightily a man came up to me tapping his wristwatch.

"How long will it take?" he asked.

He thought that the purpose of the foghorn was to blow the fog away.

One day we had a visitor who could tell me that he had travelled, on a ship, with my cousin Ian Anderson from Port Stanley in the Falkland Islands to Montevideo. Small world.

Chapter 29

Summer

ALL this time Margaret and I had been really happy together. It was the longest time we had ever had together but did not alter the fact that we lacked many of the things that households take for granted. We had no television, no carpets, no washing machine and no ready-made way of getting them.

Brian Johnson was in one day having a cup of coffee with us. He remarked, in a very tactful way, we would need some things that we did not have. Maybe he thought we could not afford to buy luxuries but he offered to take us, on a day off, to Thurso. For Margaret especially this was an exciting opportunity.

The shopping list was long and punishing to the bank account. Nonetheless it was a day to remember. In Thurso we bought many of the things that made our home a bit more user friendly. We went for carpet squares rather than fitted carpets because they could be re-used in another house. The washing machine was the very latest, state of the art model, a Hotpoint twin tub. It took the drudgery out of washing and made Margaret's life a lot easier. As for the TV, that was welcome too although we could only get one channel, BBC1. I discovered that by fiddling with the aerial on the chimney we could get ITV but we lost BBC1 in the process.

We mostly stuck with the BBC channel but every Monday there was a programme called *Strictly Scottish* featuring performers like the Jacky Sinclair Show Band. In that band was Unst musician Mackie Burns. So it became a weekly chore to go on the lum to tune in ITV with someone in the house watching the TV and another outside relaying the results of my labours. We were the only house at the station that got any ITV picture so everyone crowded into our sitting room to see this programme. Another night we had a similar houseful to see a film about the American artist Andy Warhol. On it was a profoundly unattractive female who painted "pictures" with her diminutive breasts.

At any lighthouse station inspection day was never looked forward to but it was a day I hated at Cape Wrath. The inspection itself was the least of it. All the annual stores were landed including the yearly allowance of coal and dozens of barrels of paraffin and diesel. The landing jetty took the form of a slipway and sloped into the sea. The idea was that cargo could be worked at any state of the tide. The launch from the ship was positioned alongside so the gunwale was level with the edge of the pier. The station tractor was reversed down and a chain harness buckled somewhat insecurely to the leggings of the barrels. The tractor then dragged them up to the top two at a time.

A lightkeeper drove the tractor and the other two stayed at the top to roll away the barrels and up-end them. Seamen manhandled the barrels out of the boat and coupled them to the tractor. On the face of it the tractor driver seemed to have the best job but when you came to do it that was questionable. Not every barrel was tight and some oil would leak out on to the pier making it slippery and dangerous, but that cut no ice with the seamen. No matter how fast you drove the tractor you came in for complaints and abuse from them for being too slow. The fact that the pier was none too wide and had a right angle bend in the middle helped none at all.

Unloading the coal was even worse. The coal came in large open bags that held anything up to two hundredweight. Sometimes, depending on the state of the tide, they were landed in two feet of water. It was the job of the lightkeepers to be down at the pier to load them on to the trailer. If the tractor was difficult to reverse down the slippery pier it was ten times more difficult when coupled to the trailer. For my part I was simply not strong enough to lift those soaking wet bags of coal head high into the trailer. I had to work along with another man in order to play my part.

At the top of the pier the trailer had to be emptied and this was repeated until all the coal was ashore. The very next day we had to load it all up again, take it to the station, carry it in on our backs and empty each family's quota into the individual coal sheds.

Although our finances had taken a serious blow we were determined to go home to Shetland for our holidays. We arranged the time off and booked our flight from Wick to Sumburgh. It was a delight to see our parents and friends again and we saw, in the short time that we had been away, a number of changes. Three of our best friends were building new houses. They were working together making the concrete blocks and the houses were in the early stages of construction. So pleased were they with the progress made that they hired a bus and invited us, and others, to go to the pub with them for a celebration.

It was regatta season and we were able to take in a number of events that enabled us to see many more of our friends. We only had two weeks and back at Cape Wrath the holiday was soon no more than a pleasant memory. But always something was happening at the station.

Cape Wrath is so isolated that it is nearly impossible to commute from Durness or anywhere else except in summer, so the lightkeepers and their families were required to provide the artificers with accommodation. We had nothing against the individuals concerned. They were all nice men, but there was a certain amount of resentment that this was compulsory, not open to discussion and there was no consultation regarding the timing.

It was one of the very few times that I found myself in conflict with HQ but they were unbending. The tivvies had to be housed with the keepers and there was no question of changing their routine visits. We had to accept this and just got on with it. It was during this visit by the engineers that Brian Johnson decided to apply for a job as an artificer. There was a vacancy and Brian was a time-served motor mechanic and therefore eligible for consideration. Artificers had to be able to do a great many different things but one condition was that they had to be time-served in some trade. He was supported in his application by district officer Walter Wilson.

Walter was a senior artificer and, indeed, it was he who had suggested that Brian should consider making a bid for the job. Brian's application was successful so in the fullness of time he left the Cape for good and we had a number of supernumeraries before a new assistant was appointed. I had so recently been a Super myself that I was very sympathetic towards them. Some were very good and could be relied on but others had to be watched. They could get things very wrong.

One of them came to us shortly after the ship had been with the annual stores and all the tanks were brim full of diesel. One morning I was aware of much activity in the engine room. When I went to see what was going on I found the Super working like a frantic farmer making hay on the one dry day of a wet summer. He had the entire year's supply of waste emptied out of the bags on the engine room floor. Cotton waste was rather precious. We never got that much of it so it was used sparingly. It was for cleaning engine parts and wiping hands when working with oil or grease and, of course, the tivvies used it on their visits.

What had happened was that the header tank that fed the generators with fuel oil had overflowed. It had overflowed because the Super had never shut off the valve in from the storage and, being full, it had continued to run in. How many gallons had overflowed I have no idea but the engine room was flooded and the diesel was more than an inch deep in places. No amount of waste could soak all that up. We had to open the doors and sweep it outside to soak away. The whole place stank for weeks but there was no help for it. The Super looked suitably shamefaced but Donald did not give him any severe telling off.

Another Super we had came close to a serious injury. He was from Uist and had been in the army and wore, every day, a pair of hob-nailed boots. The lawnmower we had could be difficult to start and had a habit of firing up when you least expected it. On this occasion the Super had just about given up and was probably on his final pull of the cord. The engine suddenly burst into life and his foot, braced on the cover of the blade, slipped and went underneath into the business bit of the machine. There was a loud crack and the mower promptly stalled and became silent. This was a good deal more than could be said for the Super. He came away with a string of oaths, curses and expletives that any trooper would be proud of and, looking at his foot, it was clear that his army boot had met its Waterloo. The sole had been cut neatly away from the upper and the incredibly lucky thing was that the sharp blade had made a clean pass between the sole of his foot and the sole of the boot without touching the skin. The boot was a write-off but he might well have had his toes chopped off.

Yet another Super at the Cape during this period was Jack Barclay. Jack's parents lived in New Zealand but he had come to Shetland for a visit and had decided to stay. Jack's mother came from Unst and his father was from Sandwick. Although I did not know it at the time I was to see a lot more of Jack when we were assistants at Muckle Flugga.

This period was very enjoyable because there was always someone new coming to the station. Between Supers the occasionals were in and made a welcome change to the routine. One was a stranger on a one-off visit and it was generally agreed that one visit was plenty. He was a very quiet, dour man who seemed to have little aptitude for any job that was ongoing. One day Donald asked him to paint downpipes, the pipes that drained roof water into the tanks. He needed a stepladder to reach the highest part of the pipes but he had no idea that he should take a pot of paint up the ladder with him. Instead he placed the paint close to the bottom of the ladder so that every time that he needed to dip his brush into the paint he had to descend the ladder. It took him the entire morning to paint one pipe that was no more than about eight feet long. When someone asked him if he was going to sign his painting the irony was entirely lost on him.

Bobby Morrison, the occasional keeper from Durness, was very fond of porridge but it had a rather unfortunate effect on him. It gave him severe rumble root. He would often have to go, with all the speed that he could muster, to the nearest toilet. Bobby had bad legs and his top speed was no more than a modest amble. He had a particularly bad day when we painted the stairs in the tower. They were painted with dark brown treads and cream sides. The stairs had to be useable at all time so the practice was to paint every second step which meant that, going up or down, the stairs had to be taken two at a time. It is enough to say that Bobby had had porridge for breakfast that morning!

Another incident occurred on a day when I was off and there was never a better day not to be among those present. An entire newly opened one gallon can of black paint was dropped down the stairs. It ran all the way from the lightroom to the outside door and splashed the walls on the way down. The mess was spectacular. It took the rest of the day to clean up and another day to re-paint.

In the fullness of time a new assistant was appointed. His name was Stewart Pairman. He was English but had lived in South-west Scotland for some considerable time. He was single and was ex-navy, but he very soon slotted in to the routine of the station. He had been an occasional keeper at Killantringan, near Stranraer.

This made a difference to me because I was now officially first assistant and the duties done by the junior man passed to Stewart. He, therefore, took over the cleaning of the vaporisers and the weather log and, of course, I was the man in charge if Donald was away for any reason.

I did not have long to wait before getting my opportunity to run the station. Donald and Mima went away because the birth of their second child was imminent. Stewart and I got on all right but we had some difficult and dirty jobs to do. The insides of the water tanks had to be cleaned. We could clean no more than one at a time; to drain any more than one would be to leave the station short of water to cook with. It was only when a tank was drained that I realised how filthy they were inside. I wondered if I would ever stomach water from them again. We cleaned them and, because there was no other water I, like everyone else, went back to using it again. There was never any question of drinking it anyway, it was for cooking only.

Donald phoned to tell us that the baby had been born. It was a girl and she was to be named Shirley Anne. When they arrived back at the Cape we all went to see the baby and give her little gifts. When Donald and I were out of the way a laughing Mima told Margaret about the night that Shirley Anne was born and Donald's reaction. Donald so much wanted a girl and he had got a picture in his mind of what she should look like. It was picture of perfection, an angel. When he saw her she was like all newborn infants, red, wrinkled and crying. Donald was silent and looked glum but denied that anything was wrong or that he was unhappy. After an interval he could contain himself no longer and burst out: "My God, Mima. She is ugly!"

Back at work again Donald was not entirely happy with my running of the station. The light was not as bright as it should be and he ordered all parts of it, vaporiser and Bunsen, to get a special cleaning. Perhaps Stewart was less than thorough with his cleaning or maybe there was some other reason entirely but as the man in charge it was my responsibility. It was a lesson learned.

CHAPTER 30

WINTER AGAIN

SUMMER is a short, fleeting season in a place like Cape Wrath. At last all the summer work was finished and we settled down for another winter. As the days became shorter the trips to Durness and the Cape Wrath Hotel became fewer and the routine of the station was all we had to look forward to.

A never-ending problem was damp. The dwelling houses had been built in the days when damp-proofing was unheard of and damp travelled up the walls on the inside whenever it was wet in winter. To combat the damp was near to impossible. The lack of an adequate electricity supply meant that electric heaters could not be used. We had paraffin heaters and plenty of fuel for them but they had no ability to dry the walls. In fact they seemed to make matters worse.

Donald wrote numerous letters to HQ demanding that something be done. His preferred solution would be to re-classify the station as a rock with the lightkeepers and their families living elsewhere. This happened eventually but not until Donald, and Margaret and I, had long gone.

In the meantime the board agreed to ask the environmental health department of Sutherland County Council to inspect the houses and submit a report advising whether or not they were fit to live in. The inspectors duly arrived by helicopter and the downdraft from the chopper did untold damage to the garden so painstakingly hacked out of the rough by the womenfolk.

Imagine my surprise when the first man to step out of the aircraft was Ronnie Williamson from Mid Yell, a man I knew very well indeed. He worked for the council. In those days they were called sanitary inspectors but they did the same sort of job. They had a look at all the houses but nothing very much came of it at the time.

During this period we got new neighbours. Stewart Pairman was unhappy at the Cape and wanted to get away. I did not blame him for that. He was a single man and life was a bit dull, especially in winter. The new folk were to become lifelong friends. Alan and Irene Crowe both had lighthouse pedigrees. Irene's father was the principal keeper at Kinnairds Head and her sister was married to another lightkeeper. Irene was a Shetlander from Dunrossness.

Alan came from the oldest lightkeeping family of all. In direct line the first Crowe to join the service did so in 1793. As it turned out Alan was one of the last lightkeepers. He was there to the very end and received, from Princess Anne, a parchment recognising the service given by his family. Alan and Irene have no children so Alan would have been the last of the dynasty in any event.

We did look forward, very much, to Christmas because Joan, Margaret's sister and her daughter, Alexis, had promised to come and spend the festive season with us. Joan's husband, Andrew, was a seaman and had no home leave at Christmas. When the time came John Muir, the boatman, offered to fetch them from Lairg, the nearest railway station.

John asked how he would recognise Joan and Alexis. It was never going to be a problem. Lairg is hardly King's Cross, and the number of folk leaving the train would have been in single figures. Margaret told him he was to look for a woman who looked like the Queen. That seemed to do the trick because they all arrived safely at the Cape and it was great to see them and have the opportunity of paying back some of the hospitality we had enjoyed in their house in Cults.

The weather was good given the time of year. It was quiet and mild so Alan and I had no hesitation in going to Wick Airport to fetch an item of airfreight for the lighthouse. Joan took the opportunity to impress on me to be sure and bring back Brussels sprouts to be part of the Christmas dinner. For Joan to have a Christmas dinner without Brussels sprouts was unthinkable.

John and his wife Cathy joined us for Christmas and given that we were so far away from anywhere else we had a wonderful time. Of course the work of the lighthouse had to go on with the same routine as any other time of the year but all extra work was suspended for the duration of the festive season. It seemed to be a never-ending party with the same faces all sitting around eating and drinking far too much.

New Year came and went in a blink and before we knew it time for Joan and Alexis to return to Aberdeen. We missed them greatly and were almost homesick for a time, but the year had taken the turn and the days were ever so slightly longer. In mid-January we had a blizzard. It was on a Saturday and the visibility was so bad that I had to start the foghorn mid-morning. The snow was not entirely dry and the direction of the wind meant the snow was driving straight in to the jaws of the horn. Every blast blew some of it out again but inevitably moisture began to appear on the floor of the hut that housed the siren. I was alerted to a problem when the foghorn changed note. The first second or two of every blast was normal but it would change to a high-pitched squeal.

This was something that I had never experienced before and did not know how to deal with. I was on my way to report to Donald when I met Alan. He had heard the problem and had come to see if I needed help. He was not too sure what to do either but suggested that the siren be changed. As with every other piece of lighthouse equipment there was a spare and it was stored in the engine room. A siren from a foghorn is more than half a hundredweight of solid brass. It consists of a sleeve with a turbine inside it that revolves at high speed when the compressed air is blown through it. It is precisely made and perfectly balanced, stored in a wooden box made for that purpose.

We took the wheelbarrow to the horn house, shut off the air, dismantled the housing and withdrew the siren. There was nothing at all wrong with it except that it was very wet. We installed the new siren and started it up again and it worked to perfection. But that was short-lived. In a matter of a few minutes it was failing to make a proper noise and it too was squealing and whining.

In the meantime we had dried off and lightly oiled the original one so it was ready for use again whenever it was needed. Donald took over the watch but I stayed with him in case he needed help to change the siren again because the snow showed no signs of easing. As with most other things Donald took a fairly relaxed view of the situation. Whenever the horn gave a really bad blast he would laugh and say: "That was a bloody good one!"

By the time the snow stopped we had changed the siren several times – a two-man job. All the weather equipment like the ground thermometers and rain gauge were buried deep and we had to clear an area around them so observations could be made as normal.

The spring of 1974 saw the departure of Donald and Mima from the station. Donald had tried long and hard to get away and in some measure it had become a battle of wills between him and HQ. He sent letters of complaint every week and they seemed determined to knock him back every time even when the points were valid.

The Land Rover was a good example. It was way past its sell-by date, and no-one would have been silly enough to buy it. It could never have passed an MoT test and it had no insurance. HQ pointed out that it did not need insurance because the Northern Lighthouse Board had an exemption. They had sufficient funds and were well able to settle any claim made against them.

It was clear to Alan and I that there would be no new Land Rover until Donald was transferred. He had asked for one too often and had rubbed them up the wrong way. In any event Donald had got what he wanted, a transfer to Hyskeir and they were to live in Oban. The MacAuleys were a nice family and we were sorry to see them go even though it was what they wanted.

We always remembered Donald fondly. He was always a pleasant workmate and boss and enjoyed life as best he could. Once when he had had a few refreshments he fell off the pier. It was an ebb and he landed along the rocks on his bald head. In the process he had lost his glasses. Later, when telling the story, he said: "I don't know how to hell I found my glasses without them."

Margaret was especially sorry to lose Mima as a friend. Since the day that we arrived at the Cape Mima had always been friendly towards Margaret and they enjoyed each other's company. The entire station was on tenterhooks as we waited to hear who was to be Donald's replacement. It was, in fact, another MacAuley, Alex. I knew Alex because he had been the first assistant at Rona when I was there as a supernumerary. Alex had joined the service at an older age than most so it reflected when the time came for him to be promoted. Cape was his first appointment as a principal keeper. Both he and his wife, Nancy, came from Islay and were Gaelic speakers. Alex was a quiet, placid, easy-going man who made the best of every situation. In many ways he was very different from Donald but they soon settled in. By this time, and after the arrival of the Crowes, I had gone back to being junior man, back to vaporiser cleaning and all the paperwork of the Met observations, but that how it went in the service, the luck of the draw.

With Alex in charge the morning routine was rather amusing. As always, at any station, the lightkeepers would gather in the engine room or workshop each morning. In summer it was a 9 o'clock start and in winter 10. Alan Crowe was always impatient. He wanted to be told what to do by the principal keeper and then get on with it without any delay. That was not the way that Alex worked.

Alan was a non-smoker and used to pace up and down like a caged lion while Alex and I sat on the bench and lit up cigarettes. Alex was never in a hurry and never showed any urgency about any job that needed doing. Sometimes it might be an hour or more before Alex made any mention of work. The moment he did Alan leaped into action; he would hear the last of what Alex said as he went out the door.

229

At Cape Wrath all keepers were recruited as auxiliary coastguards. There was a huge length of coastline from the Kyle of Durness and away down the west coast that was entirely empty of people. Not only that but it was a dangerous coastline so to have experienced men in the area, on call, made sense. We had a breeches-buoy, rocket gun, flares and all the equipment needed. Professional coastguards visited at regular intervals to see that we were up to speed; we did drills and exercises so that if any emergency occurred we could do what was needed until help arrived. In fact there was only one callout during my time there.

A creel boat had failed to return to Scrabster and an object had been sighted on the Cape Wrath side of the Kyle. It was the last of the daylight and observers could not determine what it was. It could have been a small boat, so we were asked to search the coast. It proved a very difficult task. It was pitch dark with a strong wind and heavy rain. We had to dress up in oilskins and rubber boots and the distance to cover was daunting. The area to search was within the bombardment range and the landscape was so pitted with shell craters it was like the surface of the moon. Every hole was full of water and you had no way of knowing whether they were a few inches or five feet deep. It was unwise to try and wade through any of them but to walk around them all added miles to the distance walked. If that was not bad enough we were tripping over shells. The Ministry of Defence always insisted that there was nothing left on the range that could explode but we never believed them and it was a brave man that ignored the dozens of sinister-looking shells that were strewn everywhere.

In the end we found nothing. We had covered the coastline from the lighthouse to the mouth of the Kyle of Durness. We all had the uneasy feeling that we may have missed something because so much of our time had been spent fighting the wind and rain and looking out for shell holes but more urgently for unexploded shells. Another difficulty was that the sea, in this area, is often a long way from the cliff face, often out of range of all but the most powerful torch.

We were stood down for the night. To get off the soaking wet clothes, get a hot drink and sit down was heaven but, of course, the watchkeeping at the lighthouse had to continue regardless. On the following day came the good news that the creel boat was safe and sound and the object seen on our side was, in fact, a lump of hawser, a towrope that had been lost from a tugboat.

CHAPTER 31

HIGH EXCITEMENT

A BIT later in the winter we heard a piece of exciting news from home. Our best friends, Gordon Jamieson and Anne Moar were to be married on 16th April and we immediately made plans for holidays so that we could be there. Gordon and I had long been friends and shared many adventures and secrets. Margaret and Anne had gone to school together and Anne and I had worked together for a time.

We knew that the wedding was coming. They had been building a new house for many months and it was just a question of picking the right time. Together they had designed their dream home. Gordon had drawn the plans, made all the concrete blocks and physically built the house up from the ground. He had worked night and day as well as doing his day job in the family coach and taxi business.

The wedding and the break that came with it was very welcome. We had scarcely been away from the Cape since our last visit to Shetland and although we never suffered from cabin fever it was, nonetheless, good to see old friends again.

Something else happened at that time to overshadow the big wedding. When we were alone together Margaret said she was as sure as she could be that she was pregnant. This news rather knocked me sideways. It was not entirely unexpected but at the same time it was hard to believe. Margaret had been aware of this for a short time and had told me as soon as she was sure. We told our parents and took every opportunity to talk to each other about this colossal event in our lives.

Our thoughts at once turned to our home at Cape Wrath. There was no question that if we asked for a transfer it would be readily granted. We were aware that we had been happy and content at Cape Wrath but everyone wanted away from the place and the fact that they were there at all was something of a misfortune.

On one day of our holiday we went across to Unst and visited the Muckle Flugga shore station. There we met Tommy Georgeson. He told us he was in the process of requesting a transfer back to the Isle of Man and reckoned that if we were to ask for a transfer to Muckle Flugga it might work to the benefit of both of us. The thinking was that Muckle Flugga was none-too-popular either and if the personnel officer had someone asking for Muckle Flugga there was some sort of a chance that it might happen. Tommy's wife was Manx and wanted very much to get back to her native island.

We went back to Cape Wrath full of thoughts of the future. I am not quite sure about Margaret but I was both excited and scared by the thought of being a parent. There was little doubt in our minds that we wanted to leave the Cape and go to Muckle Flugga. It was, again, a question of timing. If we were to move it would ideally be in the summer. The baby was due in November so we wanted to be well settled before then.

I spoke to the principal, Alex, and to Alan and both agreed that if I put in for a transfer I would get away from Cape Wrath. Not one to hang around, I took the bull by the horns and phoned Mr Dickson. During my time as a supernumerary I spoke to Mr Dickson almost on a weekly basis but as an appointed lightkeeper it was very different. I had no reason to contact him. He listened to what I had to say but gave little indication of whether or not I would be given a transfer. He said he would be in touch but that no immediate transfer would come my way; it was a matter of being patient. The conversation surprised me little. I had become used to the ways of HQ and their unwillingness to say a lot. I also knew that for me to get a transfer meant a number of others being shifted as well.

In the meantime we were somewhat unsettled. We waited and expected some news every day but nothing happened. It was about three months before Tommy Georgeson phoned from Muckle Flugga to tell me he was to be transferred to a station in the Isle of Man. For me this was half the battle. We now knew that a place was available at Muckle Flugga. Sure enough, before the morning was out Alex MacAuley came to where I was working and told me Mr Dickson was on the phone and wanted to speak to me. It was the news we wanted to hear. My transfer to Muckle Flugga was to go ahead. Not only that, but I was to pack our belongings and arrange to have them taken to Scrabster and join the *Pole Star.*

Margaret was as pleased as I was about the shift but far from happy at the prospect of travelling on the ship. Mr Dickson readily agreed that she could fly to Shetland from Wick and so all this was arranged. As it was I arrived in Shetland safe and sound after what was a rather choppy crossing of the Sumburgh Roost but Margaret was fogbound in Orkney and delayed overnight. If everything had gone according to plan she would have arrived before me but I beat her to it.

I arrived at the Muckle Flugga shore station to news of a tragedy. A young German birdwatcher had fallen to his death over the cliffs of Hermaness. Hermaness is a world-renowned bird reserve but it can be a rather dangerous place. The whole hill is dome-shaped and gets steeper all the way to the cliff face. In summer the coarse grass gets polished. The birdwatcher had slipped and fallen. The Muckle Flugga boat was launched for what they hoped was a rescue mission but turned out to be the grim task of recovering the body. All this happened a day or two before I arrived.

CHAPTER 32

LIFE AT THE NESS

MR DICKSON, true to form, had timed my arrival so that we had time to settle in before my first stint on the rock. We had a fortnight, in fact. Margaret and I both belong to Yell and with Unst being a near neighbour we knew a great many folk there. The Muckle Flugga shore station, where we lived, was referred to locally as the Ness. The houses for keepers and their families were a block of four flats. Ours was ground floor and next door to us was the principal keeper, Magnie Leask, also from Yell and his wife Margaret, originally from Islay.

Upstairs immediately above us was Jack Barclay and his wife Winifred, who is from Unst. Jack we knew already because he had been a Super at Cape Wrath before being appointed. An important fact for me was that while I was at the station I was to travel to and from the rock with the principal.

While we were at Cape Wrath some important changes had been made, one being that lightkeepers were granted a 40-hour working week. At a land station like Cape Wrath it made for a fiendishly complicated watch-keeping rota but at a rock station it meant that we worked four weeks on the rock and then had four weeks off. A relief of the rock was made every two weeks and this meant that when the principal keepeer and I went to the rock our opposite numbers came ashore, leaving a man, who had been there two weeks only, to continue. After another two weeks the next relief took one man on and one man off.

Four years had passed since I had been to Flugga as a supernumerary and all the lightkeepers had moved on. The veterans who manned the boat were still there but with one important change. Jimmy Lowrie Edwardson MBE had retired and Jonathan Wills had taken over as skipper.

Jonathan was a somewhat unlikely skipper. He was an academic, soon to get his PhD, and had the distinction of being the first student rector of Edinburgh University. In contrast to the native crew he had a 'proper' Queen's English accent that was exactly like a BBC newsreader, as he later became. As I was to find out, Jonathan was a quick learner and was always ready to ask and to take advice from the vastly experienced crew in front of him. He was also the very best of neighbours. By this time Margaret was quite heavily pregnant and we did not own a car. Jonathan never left the station without calling in to see if Margaret needed any shopping.

Jonathan was green fingered and had a beautiful garden. On fine summer mornings he was always out early tending his vegetables and flowers. Every day when we, and our neighbours, went out first thing in the morning we would find some gift from his garden on the doorstep, a lettuce, a bunch of young carrots or whatever. It was very welcome.

When we had settled I was expected to act as the 'lightkeeper ashore' which meant that while most of the time was my own I was still expected to do certain duties at the shore station. If any of the keepers on the rock wanted to make a phone call I had to connect them to an outside line. Also there

were the routine 'speaks' that took place three times a day to confirm that all was well on the rock.

Keepers ashore were expected to do the maintenance work like painting and lime washing. Being the last week in August nearly all that work had been done but the roofs had never been tarred. The roof of the main building was flat with a low safety wall around it. Jack Barclay and I set about this one fine day. The tar we were using was rather thick and should have been warmed but we just poured it out by the gallon and spread it with old floor brushes. It seemed to work and no-one ever looked at it or said we had done the wrong thing.

It was on 26th August that I went to Muckle Flugga for the first time as an appointed lightkeeper. Not only that but I was the senior assistant, deputy to the principal. In contrast to my first landing this was flat calm, a ladies' landing. With me was Magnie Leask, principal keeper.

After stowing away the ropes we joined John Henry Priest in the kitchen. John was a new breed of lightkeeper. He and others like him were classed as local assistants. Since the coming of the 40-hour week more men were needed. A local assistant was employed full time but was never expected to move to any other lighthouse. For them the down side was that if their lighthouse was automated they had no job. John was always referred to by both his first names. I knew John Henry before but when I lived with him on Muckle Flugga I got to know him a lot better and he became a great friend and maybe the best rock mate I ever had.

Bertie Mathewson (left) sorting out the mail as attending boatman Lowrie Edwardson steers the Grace Darling *out to 'Da Rock' in the summer of 1974.*
© Jonathan Wills

Now that I was stationed at Flugga I had the opportunity and the need to learn all about the workings of the place. I had to know it all because if I was ever left in charge knowing how things worked was a must and, without a doubt, the station was complicated.

Much money had been spent on the place. The Northern Lighthouse Board seemed to look on Britain's most northerly lighthouse as some kind of status symbol. In the 1960s as well as the building of the new accommodation block the rock itself had been reinforced. The shore side of Muckle Flugga is layered and sloping. There was some danger of slippage so a firm called Allens had been given the contract to stabilise the rock structure. Deep holes were bored into the rock and massive rawl bolts inserted. To complete the job a new stairway was built. The old stone steps were badly worn but the new stairway was aluminium and constructed in flights of about 12 to 15 steps each with walkways between them. This served a dual purpose. If someone fell on the stairs it meant they could not go all the way to the bottom, only down one flight, and it allowed the stairway to take the easiest route to the top.

Chapter 33

Learning Muckle Flugga

LEARNING the routine of the station was not good enough. I also had to learn all the quirks of the various bits and pieces. I thought I knew all about the generators because they were the same as the ones at Cape Wrath but they, too, were overloaded and leaked oil and were ultra bad to start.

After an overhaul they were better for a time until someone would use 'easy start'. It came in a spray can and certainly helped but once it was used the engines seemed to get hooked on it and you had to use it every time. There were no self-starters and sometimes by the time you got them going, using the handle, you felt like going to bed.

The plumbing was very complex. The main pump that took water in to the Braithwaite tanks in the quarterdeck from the outside tanks was not, in fact, a pump. It was an impeller and the whole system was subject to airlocks. It was multi-functional and could move the water to wherever it had to be put. It was vitally important to open and close the many valves in the correct order otherwise nothing happened and you could spend hours getting rid of the airlocks and getting the system primed again. Rainwater was saved and used to flush the toilet and wash clothes. However, much of the plumbing was stainless steel so salt water could be used in an emergency. Fresh water had to be taken from the shore in plastic barrels and hoisted up on the Blondin wire. This worked in exactly the same way as a cable car and was a really efficient way of taking cargo from the boat up to the top of the cliff. In summer it was never a problem to land cargo but in the winter good enough weather for landing cargo was rare.

Of course we used water sparingly but never had enough to last all winter. In the autumn every opportunity was taken to top up the tanks but even so supplies would be running low come the New Year. Looking back at the diaries it seemed that a weather window usually appeared early in February.

It was vitally important to keep an adequate supply of food on the rock. The NLB paid lightkeepers a daily allowance and this was used for whatever was needed. The man in charge had overall responsibility for everything but it was common practice for the first assistant to look after the food stocks.

Almost all our groceries were bought from Alex Priest's shop in Burrafirth. It was the nearest shop to the shore station and they were always helpful. Alex was a tailor. He had been trained after the First World War when he was badly wounded rescuing a comrade under fire. For this act of bravery he had been awarded the Military Medal.

His shop had started as tailor's but over time evolved into a general store. Alex was now retired but was in the shop most days and was always popular with customers. For a small shop like this the lighthouse and the families attached to it were the biggest customers, but this was something of a double-edged sword. The shop had to wait three months to get paid. The principal keeper would collect the bills and send them to the lighthouse board with all the rest of the quarterly returns.

At the rock, as first assistant, I kept a pad in the kitchen and compiled a list of items required from the shop. Other keepers would add to it. We often had extra mouths to feed when we had workmen on the rock. We were entitled to charge them for their keep. There was a recognised fee that they all paid. The allowance paid by the board was enough but the more men we had on the rock the easier it was to make ends meet.

We bought meat in bulk and if we had any surplus money we used to give to Maggie Edwardson to take to the NAAFI shop in the RAF base. The shop was not open to the public but Maggie worked there and would get some things that were not in the local shops. We got large catering-sized tins of coffee and various different bottles of pickle and chutney that were looked on by us as luxuries.

The diesel arrived in barrels and had to be emptied and pumped to the header tanks that fed the generators. As well as being run in turns there was a strict routine for maintenance. The number of hours that each engine ran was logged and the oil was changed regularly.

Towards the end of my time at Muckle Flugga the diesel was pumped up to the top, but not without difficulty. Superintendent Graham Simpson wanted to try pumping to cut out an awful lot of hard work man-handling heavy barrels. A tank full of diesel was taken to the rock in one of the ship's launches and a hose hauled all the way up the cliff. When pumping started nothing happened for a time except that the engine was labouring. No diesel ever appeared at the top but we saw the oil spurting into the air and gushing down the cliff. The hose had burst. This we fixed but the same thing happened again and the whole idea was about to be written off as a failure when Mr Simpson remembered that there was a second pump on the *Pole Star* and ordered that to be brought ashore. Four men carried it, with great difficulty, to a ledge halfway up the cliff and the hose was cut and both ends connected to this secondary pump. Both pumps were started and this time the pumping worked perfectly.

If an engine broke down, and this was not unusual, we would phone HQ and they would always ask if we could fix it. Sometimes we could and sometimes we could not but if we took on the job we got paid extra. There were no prizes for saying that we could do it and then finding we had bitten off more than we could chew. In that case they had to send men from Edinburgh. As well as the extra cost it meant the loss of valuable time. As well as the generators an understanding of the electrical system was needed. All the alternators were wired up to a central switchboard so each generator could be put on load or isolated.

It was also important to know where everything was kept. If any lightkeeper had a problem in the middle of the night he would always try to fix it himself rather than call out another man so to know where to find spare parts was useful. On really bad winter nights it was easy to get soaked to the skin when venturing outside.

The engine room was not connected to the lighthouse so to check the generators keepers had to go outside. The cliffs on the north side of Muckle Flugga are sheer and with heavy seas waves crash into the cliff and the spray falls on top by the ton. No-one is any danger of being washed away because of the walls and railing along the cliff edge. That said, any mistimed run between the two carried the certainty of the most comprehensive soaking imaginable. It was routine for the man going off watch to go to the engine room to make a final check before handing over.

On one particular night when I was taking over from Magnie he asked me if I knew how to time the run. When I said no he offered to show me. We both went to the porch and looked out. It was 10pm and dark but the outside lights showed something of what was happening. Every now and then there would be a bang and a shudder and the deluge of seawater would descend with a roar and a loud swoosh. Magnie explained that the sea was so bad he had opened a window on the lee side of the engine room and rigged a step so we could go in and out the window without having to use the door on the weather side. He further explained that every fourth wave was bigger than the rest so the trick was to wait until it had been and gone and then make your run. We watched several lots of four and, sure enough, it seemed to be the case.

"I am going after the next one," he said.

He got halfway when the biggest wave of the night struck and Magnie disappeared in the torrent only to emerge again like a ewe newly out of the annual dipping. I was not sure whether it was safe to laugh because at first I did not know if he was alright, but other than being soaked he was none the worse.

Another routine job for lightkeepers in the summer was cleaning the Comb, the landing area. With warm weather it got covered with green slime that was very slippery. Rigging or taking in the mooring ropes with bad weather was a tricky enough job at the best of times and to have secure footing was vital. The cleaning agent used was oxalic acid. It came in the form of white powder which was mixed with water and scrubbed into the rock with hard brushes and was particularly effective when the rock was dry and the sun shining. To keep the Comb clean this had to be done every two weeks or so all summer.

Muckle Flugga is only one part of a larger series of skerries. Beyond the landing place is the Peerie Flugga and near the steps up is a narrow sound between Muckle Flugga and Cliff Skerry. It is only a few yards wide and a wire had been stretched across and suspended below it was a seat like a bosun's chair so it was possible to cross. This led to other skerries all joined together, including the Rumblings, where there is a large gannet colony. Off duty a pleasant afternoon could be spent there but we always went in twos for safety reasons.

It is a wise man who knows everything but gradually I learned the complexities of the rock and felt there was no situation I could not deal with. In terms of recreation there were two workshops well equipped with tools, including turning lathes, and materials where keepers could while away their own time, not that there was very much. Some conjure up visions of lightkeepers with white whiskers whittling away at pieces of wood or putting ships in bottles and while this may be partly true the routine of keeping a watch around the clock seven days a week with housekeeping duties and keeping everything spotless and in apple pie order took a lot of time.

One of the workshops was referred to as the smithy. In bygone days that is exactly what it was, but in my time it was the wood store and where woodworking was done. Another building was the henhouse. Again it was disused. The practice of keeping hens had been abandoned because the poor unfortunate birds kept blowing away.

Muckle Flugga was a mass of buildings. When the new accommodation block was built they also built what was supposed to be a temporary cookhouse. It was never demolished and became the paint and rope store and was entirely suitable for that purpose.

On a place so exposed nothing could be left outside, so a small hut had been built, a lean-to on the kitchen, to keep butane gas containers in. There was the red light hut, the red light being a fixed light that guarded the dangerous east coast of Unst. Alongside that was the winch house with the engine that hauled the cargo up the Blondin wire.

My first time on the rock was one of contrasting emotions. On the one hand I was learning what was essentially a new job but on the other hand I was away from Margaret. Admittedly she had the freedom to go and stay with her parents but she was trying to set up our house at the Ness as a home and she had no car. I spoke to her daily on the VHF and she kept assuring me she was OK, but nonetheless I was slightly concerned for her wellbeing. In any event, I was glad to get back to the shore and see her again. Since we had married three years before this we had, in contrast to our courting days, never been apart. I also knew that I would have to go Flugga for another stint before the baby was born.

Chapter 34

PARENTHOOD

LITTLE did I know how traumatic it would be when the time came. As a first-time father-to-be I was nervous in the extreme. It was very fashionable, at the time, for fathers to watch the birth of the baby. I was not at all sure if I wanted to be there because I knew I could not do anything very useful. Margaret said she would like me to be with her so it was decided, but that is not how it worked out.

I sat at her bedside for four days watching her become weaker and feeling worse and worse but no baby arrived or looked likely to arrive. Mr Cumming, the surgeon, was called on the Friday afternoon and said that if nothing happened during the night he would operate in the morning.

Nothing changed so Margaret was prepared for theatre and there was no longer any question of me seeing the baby being born, not that this was any concern at the time. I had a mighty anxious wait but eventually a nurse came and told me that a baby girl had been delivered.

My first glimpse of my daughter came when another nurse hurried past with a red object wrapped in foil like a Sunday roast ready for the oven. I was assured that the baby was fine but was being put into an incubator because of some minor breathing difficulty. Margaret had still not come out of the anaesthetic. When she did she was in a state of some stress. She had expected to find a baby beside her and jumped to the conclusion that something awful had happened

I was told I could go and see the baby and among the other babies newly born I had no difficulty in picking out my daughter because she has the same gap between her big toe and the one next to it as I do. In due course Margaret met the newcomer too. We had already decided that if it was a girl we would call her after her grandmothers so she was named Elizabeth Anne.

I stayed in Lerwick as long as I could but I soon had to go back to work. Needless to say, I did not want to leave Margaret and Elizabeth but I left comforted by the fact that all was well and they would stay with Margaret's folk until I came back next time. And so I landed on Muckle Flugga again in good heart and basking in the congratulations and good wishes of my friends.

The next time I was home was for Christmas and the New Year. It was the way it worked out. Over time things evened themselves out. The lighthouse had to be manned festive season or no festive season and everyone accepted this as the fortunes of war. We spent Christmas with Margaret's folk in Gloup but the time was ruined because we all got a stomach bug that kept the bathroom busy all the time.

Elizabeth proved to be a handful too. She was not a good sleeper. My parents and others who knew me were quick to point out that I was exactly the same when I was her age. That knowledge was of little use either to me or Margaret and Margaret suffered from the lack of sleep herself, a state of affairs that was to continue until Elizabeth was nearly two years old. She was as happy as Larry as long as she had company but if left on her own she was grumpy.

CHAPTER 35

MAGNIE LEASK

LIFE on the rock was much easier and Magnie and John Henry proved to be the very best of rock mates. Magnie spent any spare time he had making fun. He could get a tune out of any instrument that came his way and was forever writing songs. You always had to be alert because he was an inveterate practical joker.

He had two dummies, Boki and Grülie, and they appeared in the most unlikely places. One night when I was going up the tower to the lightroom one of the dummies gave me a big fright. When I opened the door at the bottom of the stairs Boki fell into my arms. Magnie had removed the light bulb so that I had no warning.

Another time he fixed Boki on the stairs, again with the light bulb removed, but this time a piece of string connected the dummy to the door so that when the door was opened the dummy came rumbling down the steep stairs. The other dummy, Grülie, was a stepladder wearing a greatcoat and rubber boots. The head was a hard plastic float with a lightkeeper's hat. At a distance it looked quite realistic and one day when the relief boat was taking out cargoes of water Magnie placed the dummy at the rail overlooking the landing area. This is a long way away and from the boat it looked for all the world like a real man.

At the time there was an electrician working on Flugga, a man that Lowry, the boatman, did not like, and he assumed the dummy was the electrician. Every time they came out Lowry would swear for him.

"See dat lazy bugger," he would say. "Could he no help wi da barrels?"

No-one ever put him right and the next time they came out the dummy had not moved.

"Aa my God he's still dere. Does da lazy bastard hae nae wark ta du?"

That incident happened before I arrived but to Magnie it was so funny he had to wipe away the tears telling me about it. Magnie had far more ploys up his sleeve than just the dummies.

John Henry was always willing to do what was asked of him but he hated to be hurried. He politely asked Magnie to be sure and give him plenty of warning when the boat was coming. Magnie did no such thing. John was busy in the kitchen and Magnie came in and told him to hurry up because the boat was nearly here and they only had a few minutes to rig the ropes. None too pleased, John made what speed he could and tried to put on his boots. This proved to be far from easy because Magnie had stuck them to a square of plywood with strong glue. To get them clear took no end of effort and the liberal use of what might be called colourful language. When he got the boots on and went outside he found, of course, that the boat had not yet left the shore.

Another time when John Henry was cook Magnie went into the kitchen and put a teaspoonful of long grain rice into the soup. This was for the benefit of the third lightkeeper, who was very fussy about his food. If he believed that any food was less than perfect he would not touch it. They all began to sup the delicious home-made soup but Magnie, every time he found a grain of the half-cooked rice, would lay it up on the edge of his plate.

"What is it that you are finding in the soup, Magnie?" he was asked.

The grains of rice looked exactly like small maggots.

"I'm no sure," Magnie answered, "but I dunna lik da look o' it."

He carried on eating but the other man went and emptied out his soup and could eat no more at that meal. This kept Magnie chuckling all the next week.

Another consequence of the 40-hour week was that each rock station had two principal lightkeepers. They never saw each other except at the reliefs and sometimes they had different ideas about how a station should be run. Magnie was a bit of a hoarder. Anything that was thrown away had to be very useless indeed.

By contrast his opposite number was always trying to tidy up. In the workshop there were a number of boxes full of bits and pieces. Any lightkeeper doing a bit of DIY would often find something in them to help with the job. The other principal keeper would clear out the workshop and throw the contents of the boxes over the cliff. Magnie, when he returned, would set himself the task of bringing it all back. He was very slim and fit and an expert cragsman and every day he was climbing down the cliffs fetching all the stuff that had been thrown away. By the time that his month on the rock was done 90 percent of it had been recovered and put back in the boxes.

In the kitchen we had a broken table knife that had been ground down and made into a fine paring knife. One day when I was the cook I accidentally threw it over the cliff along the potato peelings. Magnie saw what had happened, dropped over the edge and disappeared. He was away for some considerable time but when he reappeared he held up the knife. All this was possible because the cliffs were not sheer except for a section on the north side.

As well as all his other qualities Magnie was a great man for telling stories. He remembered all the lighthouse happenings and told me about a great many incidents that had happened before I was there. Once when the *Grace Darling* was tied up at Muckle Flugga the weather looked like it was going to become nasty. All hands made what speed they could to get the boat away again but they discovered, to their horror, that a rope's end had been wound up by the propeller and until that was cleared movement was impossible. To get help from the shore or a diver was out of the question and they were entirely dependent on their own resources. Magnie remembered that there was a blade for a Scots scythe in the workshop which had escaped the purges. It was quickly fixed on to a long pole with jubilee clips and taken down to the landing. Peter Sinclair, the engine driver, volunteered to try and cut away the offending rope. He stripped to the waist and while other members of the crew held his feet and legs he went down, head and shoulders under the water and hacked at the rope. When he kicked his legs that was the signal that he could hold his breath no longer and he was pulled up and given a breather. Every time that he was down he made some progress and eventually he managed to free the propeller. They were thus able to get away safely from the rock and Peter was none the worse for his valiant effort.

Once when a sling broke the lightkeepers lost their personal boxes. That would very disappointing at any time of the year but this was a few days before Christmas and in the boxes were all sorts of Christmas treats that they did not have at other times of the year. One lightkeeper lost, among other things, his razor. He never bought another one and has had a beard ever since.

One other time the boat had a fire on board and, of course, reliefs had to be abandoned, cargo was lost and there were breakdowns. Magnie recorded all those things and made a monopoly type board game with all the hazards and helps that were part and parcel of serving Muckle Flugga and the men who worked there.

In the service was a lightkeeper called Jake McVittie. Magnie had met him somewhere and had quite a few stories about him. McVittie was a great character. He used to work in the shipyards and had a fierce Glasgow accent. By contrast the head of the radio department in Granton was an Englishman, Mr Roe, who had a very cultured public school accent.

Once at a remote rock station where the landing was difficult the radio beacon broke down and was sending out no signal. Mr Roe and another artificer came to fix it but had to leave again, because of the weather, with the beacon still out of action. After they had gone Jake had a look at it and removed the cover of a junction box that was fixed on the wall outside. It was crammed full of earwigs and they were shorting out the system. When they were cleared out the beacon worked fine. In triumph, the following day, Jake phoned Mr Roe to tell him the good news and he was delighted.

Peerie Willie Mathieson, Stourigarth, and his cousin Willie Gibby Mathieson, Upperhouse, Buddabrake, heading out of Burrafirth for the Flugga in the summer of 1974. © Jonathan Wills

"Jolly good show, Mr McVittie. What was the problem?"

"Horney gollachans, Mr Roe," Jake replied. "Thoosends ida bastards!"

On another occasion Jake phoned to tell Mr Roe that the storage batteries would not hold a charge.

"Perhaps they have become porous Mr McVittie."

"Aye, yer right there, Mr Roe. They're as poor as piss!" was the reply.

Magnie told me of a lighthouse that was always late lighting up. It was one that could be seen and monitored by a number of other stations. When this came to the ears of the superintendent in Edinburgh he felt he had to have a word.

The principal at this errant lighthouse was a senior lightkeeper who was due to retire quite soon. When the superintendent asked what he had to say for himself he readily conceded that sometimes they were a bit late in the afternoons. "But, by golly, we are the first ones to put out the light in the mornings!"

There was one time, Magnie told me, when NATO was exercising in the North Atlantic and requested a daily weather report from the lightkeepers at Muckle Flugga. They wanted to know wind speed, direction and visibility.

The lightkeeper on watch compiled the report and radioed it to the man ashore who relayed it to Lerwick Coastguard. One morning it was Lowry, the boatman, who took the message. As always there were a lot of eager listeners all over the island. The two men had a general conversion before Lowry said.

"I tink du better gie me dy report. Whit ert is da wind?"

"It's south-east," replied the keeper.

"Hoo muckle o it ir dae?" was the next question.

"Weel tae tell da truth it's flat calm," came the answer.

For a few seconds there was a pregnant silence before the predictable explosion.

"My God man du canna tell dem dat. Du canna tell dem a lok o shite!"

There was never a dull moment with Magnie except when it came time to waken him for his watch. It was seldom my problem because as first assistant I always followed him. He wakened me rather than the other way around. However, a sounder sleeper I never saw and to get him fully conscious took no little effort.

When we were ashore together we lived next door to each other and had a very neighbourly relationship. Magnie and his wife Margaret had two sons, Harold and Erlend. At this time they were still at primary school. Erlend was mad keen on playing games of soldiers and was seldom seen without his wooden rifle.

Whenever I ventured outdoors I would find myself under arrest. I would be prodded in the back by the muzzle of the gun, made to stand up against the wall, legs wide apart and mercilessly frisked. If I made all the correct responses I might be allowed to go on my way, but sometimes not.

Once I came under so much suspicion that I was held in custody, locked in the coal shed. When I allowed this to happen I did not realise that I really was locked in. There was no way of opening the door from the inside. At first I was not too concerned because I thought Erlend would soon let me out again. Not so. His mother called him in for his tea after which he sat down to watch the TV. He had forgotten all about me. It was only when Margaret had made our evening meal that she began to wonder where I was. It was only when she went into the Leask's house to see if I was there that Erlend remembered that

I was locked away. Everyone apologised but the expression on Magnie's face told me that inwardly he was saying: "That's my boy!"

It came as no great surprise that when he grew up Erlend made a career in the army and became one of the very best marksmen in Britain.

CHAPTER 36

Big Changes

WE WERE well settled as a family at the Ness. Elizabeth was a delightful child but was never able to sleep all night and Margaret was, more often than not, short of sleep herself. She had made friends with Mrs Leask and the Wills family. Magnus Wills was a toddler and took a lot of watching. Jonathan had fixed rabbit wire on the gates to keep him in the enclosure around the dwelling houses, otherwise he would crawl out through the bars of the metal gates.

Something that all lightkeepers and their families had to get used to was the fact that changes were never far away. Nonetheless it came as a disappointment when Magnie Leask told us he had been transferred to Sumburgh Head. He had been his time at Flugga and Sumburgh was seen as good move.

It was an Orkney man and his family that replaced the Leasks. Tommy Budge and his wife Thelma came from South Ronaldsay. They were a large family. The two eldest daughters had left home. Pam was in Edinburgh and Moira was in the Isle of Man. With Tommy and Thelma was young Tommy, aged 12, Sandra, 10, and Graham, 8. They were experienced lighthouse folk and quickly settled into the routine.

Tommy was in his late thirties. He was a man of medium height and medium build. He had jet-black hair and a neatly trimmed beard. This contrasted with his skin which was as pale as pale could be and never changed colour or took on a tan.

As with Magnie and myself Tommy and I travelled together to the rock and Margaret and Thelma readily made friends. The Budge children were a great help with Elizabeth and spent a lot of time with her. It was only when we were on the rock together that I got to know Tommy. He was a very different man from Magnie but a very pleasant companion. In some ways he was far better because he did not have all Magnie's trickery and I never felt the need to be so vigilant. It was Tommy's first station as principal so in some ways it was a learning experience for him too.

It was no time after the arrival of the Budge family that Jonathan Wills told us he was leaving. He was taking up a job as a journalist, a reporter for *The Shetland Times* newspaper, the one weekly publication that all Shetland relied on as the main source of news. This meant that the job of boatman was vacant and for us lightkeepers it was vitally important that we get the right man. At the same time we knew that we would be given no say in who was appointed. A number of names were bandied about but in the end it was a local man who got the job, Aly Sinclair. Although I did not know Aly everyone who did know him was happy. He was given the seal of approval. In any event he seemed to slot seamlessly into the job and, like Jonathan before him, his crew had plenty of experience.

In calling reliefs the onus was very much on the lightkeeper in charge on the rock. It was unacceptable to call out the boat and crew unless there was a realistic chance of making the relief. The boatman would never refuse to turn out but when they got to the landing the boatman made the final decision. If he deemed it unsafe the relief would be aborted and everyone would go home again. In practice this almost never happened because any competent lightkeeper knew what was possible and what was not. Besides, calling a relief that was unlikely to happen caused a lot of unnecessary work. At the shore end the crew had to be called, the boat had to be launched and loaded up with the stores and at the lighthouse the keepers had to rig all the ropes and stand by. If the relief proved impossible the whole procedure had to be reversed.

Another newcomer was junior assistant Lawrence Johnstone. While Jack Barclay was in the flat above us Lawrence was in the flat above the Budges. His father was from Edinburgh and his mother from South Africa. Lawrence and I were on opposite routines. He travelled to and from the rock with the other principal, Willie Gauld. This meant that I saw them only at the reliefs. Lawrence quickly became a very popular member of the team and the community ashore. All the children eagerly awaited his return from the rock because he always had home-made tablet and sweets for them.

I never did get to know Willie Gauld but although I saw very little of him I could not avoid being amazed at how small he was. He wore tiny little boots and one day, at the relief, he got his feet tangled in a rope and came into the boat headfirst. He was about to land on his head in the bottom of the boat but I put out my arms and I could not believe how light he was. It was like holding a baby.

CHAPTER 37

JOHN HENRY PRIEST

OF ALL the workmates I had in my nine years as a lightkeeper I had more fun and more laughs with John Henry Priest than anyone else. He was a brilliant rock mate. Tommy Budge used to say that if anyone could overhear us on Flugga they would think that we were three idiots because we never stopped laughing.

Of course we had our differences and occasionally harsh words were spoken but that was always by whoever it was that was on the wrong end of a trick. We did have to get used to Tommy's eating preferences. He was somewhat fussy about his food. There were a number of ordinary dishes that he did not like and most things had to be overcooked before they were to his liking.

Of course I quickly saw this as an opportunity to have a bit of fun. Everything that I knew Tommy did not like I told John was his favourite food and everything he did like I told John on no account to offer because Tommy would be mad.

John was a man who did everything slowly and you could be forgiven for thinking that he was slow-witted as well, but it took a good man to get the better of him in any sort of verbal joust.

He was as sharp as a tack and never short of a ready answer. He was quick to tumble to the fact that I was telling him lies.

But he did not know what to believe and what not to believe. One morning John was cooking the breakfast, bacon and eggs, and enquired of Tommy: "Am I right in thinking that you like your egg hard fried?"

"No, no, no," said Tommy. "Not hard, f...... rigid."

John seemed a bit crestfallen at the severity of the answer but Tommy got an egg that was like the blade of an angle grinder. A night of two after that John was at his wit's end to know what to make for Tommy's supper. Tommy was on the ten to two watch and as usual was having a sleep.

The man going off watch at this time always prepared supper. Often it would be anything left over from dinner but on this night there was nothing. I told John to make him gruel, knowing full well that this was one of Tommy's pet hates. For a good job John knew this too.

He said to me: "Man he widna aet dat no even if I made it f...... rigid!"

Tommy and John were both fond of oatcakes, but not the same sort. Tommy liked the thin Orkney ones. He would spread one with butter, put another on top, spread that with butter and put another one on top of that so he ate three at a time. John, on the other hand, liked the thick brunnies that were made in the Voe bakery.

One day Tommy demanded to sample these Voe oatcakes that John thought so much of. I fetched a packet from the larder but it was a different sort and they were even thinner than the Orkney ones. John's face was a picture when he saw them because he had always flagged up how thick they were.

Before either Tommy or I had time to say anything John said: "Sink me. Johnson an Wood is surley gone metric!"

Anyone that John thought was stupid he would refer to as being a Noddy. Once I made a set of yarn winds. I had taken care and was very pleased with my efforts. They were made from recycled white oak and looked good, so much so that I invited John and Tommy to come to the workshop to inspect my handiwork. Tommy was generous in his remarks but John never spoke to me at all but shook his head and said to Tommy: "Just da tweatings o' a Noddy."

John was good at any sort of craftwork. He used to carve wood and was also a good engineer. He made a footstool from wood and upholstered it with foam rubber and leather cloth. He would sit back watching the TV with his feet on the stool, the picture of contentment. He had a habit, when he crossed his legs, of kicking his feet in the air. Sitting alongside him I used to watch for this happening and then I would take the stool away so that his heels would come down on the hard floor with a bang. He would look daggers and sometimes make for me with the back of his hand and say: "Damn de, Lowry Tulloch. Do maks me feel wicked."

John had a delightful way of telling a story and a unique turn of phrase. He told me once that when he worked in Baltasound his boss sent him to the *Earl of Zetland* to ship out two raw cow skins. It was after hours and John knew full well that the purser would never accept them. Equally he knew that his boss would be not too pleased if he came back with them.

He never asked the purser but rolled the skins to the edge of the pier and over. They fell on the deck with a thud but John knew that the skins were too heavy to put back on the pier without some sort of a power lift. The purser heard the noise and came on the scene. I asked John if he was mad.

"Man he banged in til a horroration just lik a f...... sauvage."

Like myself John liked his food and on Muckle Flugga there was plenty – too much, if the truth be told. Among other things in the larder was a whole case of tins of pilchards. They were big, flat, oval tins with enough fish in them to feed four people if they were put in a salad, and more if they were made into sandwiches.

Once we had a supernumerary working with us. Bob Dagget was from the north of England. He was a good cook but hated pilchards and found it hard to believe that John and I were fond of them. One night Bob decided to put us to the test and served a pilchard concoction for supper. He had a big pie dish two-thirds full of mashed potatoes. On top of that he put the contents of a whole tin full of pilchards, tomato sauce and all on top and then covered it with a ridiculous quantity of strong, cheddar cheese grated and melted under the grill.

"If you eat all that I'll eat my hat," said Bob and sat back to watch.

It was enough to feed six and I was about to say so when John gave me a hard kick under the table. He pulled the dish towards him, drew a line with the edge of the serving spoon across the melted cheese and spooned exactly half of it onto his plate. He then pushed the dish towards me. By this time I had got the message and took the other half. To eat all that was stupid but we both cleaned up our plates and the look on Bob's face was, at the time, worth it. It upset my stomach and the next morning I asked John how he had fared. He said that he was so full that he was frightened to fall asleep. He felt that if he did he would roll out of the bed.

Another Super we had was far from energetic. If John or I made a cup of tea he would accept his but when he had finished he would set his cup down on the floor and wait for one of us to pick it up. There was never any question of him offering to make tea or do anything else without being told.

As the man in charge I knew I had to address this but was hoping against hope that he would snap out of it and become a team player. After a two days John came to me and angrily demanded that I sort out this 'lazy bugger'. I said to John that he was to be patient. Maybe this guy was homesick, or maybe he did not understand our language. Give him time.

"OK," said John grudgingly. "A'll no flite bit a'm gjaan tae axe him whit his last servant died o."

At that time an important figure on the world stage was the hard-line Israeli Prime Minister Menachem Begin. He was much in the news partly because of his uncompromising attitude to peace talks. Readers may well ask why he appears in this story. One day when I was the cook we had really nice meat left over from a beef roast. John wanted me to make it into a curry but I refused. I thought the meat would be better sliced, re-heated and served with gravy. Besides I much prefer a curry made from scratch. John was very persistent until I told him in no uncertain terms that I was not going to curry the beef. A moment later I overheard him saying to Tommy: "Better wid I tak on ta negotiate wi Menachem Begin!"

On Muckle Flugga there were plenty of rough seas to be seen, especially in winter. The biggest sea I ever saw was in September one year. Sitting at the table in the kitchen you do not, normally, see the sea but this particular morning I saw a giant wave going past. When we looked out the sea was breaking all the way across from the rock to the cliffs below

Saxa Vord. The three of us, John, Tommy and me went up to the lightroom to watch the sea. After watching for awhile John said it was like being in the middle of a "hell's monster of a fried egg".

Once when I was on shore they had a supernumerary on Flugga that I never saw. Out of curiosity I asked John what he was like and how they got on with him.

"Ower weel," was the non-committal reply.

It was quite clear to me, knowing John as I did, that something about this young man was not to his liking, so I asked a few more questions. After some time he said again: "He wus ower weel bit he ute da tatties wi der sheens on lik da grumpie!"

CHAPTER 38

SUPERS AND VISITORS

IT WAS December and a bright and sunny day for the time of year. It was also windy. The day started as a very ordinary one. Jack Barclay was cook. Tommy Budge and I went out after breakfast to do routine work. All the old generators in the engine room leaked both fuel oil and engine oil and every drip tray and bucket was full to the brim. Normally this waste oil would have been disposed of, burned, every week but we had had so much wind and rain that the job had never been done. This day was dry so Tommy suggested we take the opportunity to get rid of it. We were not allowed to dump waste oil over the cliff for obvious reasons. It had to be burned.

For this purpose we had a barrel on the north point. To go there we followed a narrow path that led down the slope. Tommy was in front of me carrying two five-gallon drums that, with the tops cut off and a handle fitted, served as buckets. On his feet he was wearing a pair of wooden-soled Scholl sandals.

On the path he trod on a round stone about the size of a golf ball. It rolled away under the sole of the sandal and Tommy fell on his back and got splattered with black oil. I knew immediately by the expression on his face that he was hurt. But that was confirmed at once when he said: "Please don't laugh at me. I think I have broken my leg."

I called Jack and we lifted him up, with an arm around our shoulders we took him inside to the sitting room. I left Jack to look after him and hurried to phone the shore and get help. Mercifully the sea state was good enough that the boat could come off and make a landing. Unst GP Robert Robertson agreed to come to the rock to attend to Tommy.

There was not a lot that Jack and I could do to make Tommy comfortable. He was in considerable pain but it was not unbearable. After what seemed an age the boat appeared off Sharps Point and I went down to the landing myself to put out the ropes. After the *Grace Darling* was tied up the doctor and I made our way to the top.

Tommy was given a pain-killing injection and Dr Robertson confirmed that his leg was broken. The break was in the middle of his shin, both bones, and he had to be evacuated to hospital as soon as possible. After an inflatable splint was fitted we then addressed the problem of how we were going to get him into the boat. Dr Robertson made it entirely clear that he was attending as a doctor. He had done what he could, but he would play no part in getting Tommy into the boat. We had among the emergency equipment a stretcher of the type used in mountain rescue and with helicopters. We had a look at it and decided it was no use for our purpose, it was quite simply too difficult to use on the steps. As senior man I had the responsibility and, as I saw it, there was only the one way to get Tommy down the cliff.

I went and talked to Tommy, just the two of us. I explained the problem but, of course, he knew already and had anticipated the question I was about to ask him. I needed to know if he would be prepared to allow himself to be lowered down on the cargo hoist. He said that he would go on the Blondin cable on one condition and that was if I was at the controls and did it myself. I promised him I would. I went out and renewed every rope on the cargo box. It was a heavy wooden box with ropes from each corner. There was nothing wrong with the ropes but I renewed them anyway.

The responsibility hung heavily on me. Tommy was my friend. He was badly hurt, and one tiny mistake by me could cost him his life. With the run of the mill cargo things went wrong from time to time – a sling could break, if the sling was too long it could get caught in the grating and if cargo was lowered too fast it could crash into the stop at the bottom and spill into the sea.

This time there must be no mishaps. Nothing could be left to chance. The cargo was far too precious. We fixed a seat in the box and helped Tommy in. He was in no way comfortable but it was all we could do. In the winch room I engaged the clutch and lifted the box with Tommy in it up off the ground. Jack pushed down the lever that allowed the runners to move down the cable. I shall never forget Tommy's face when he bravely waved to me as he dangled 220 feet above the bottom of the cliff. I never felt less relaxed in my life but I knew that I had to have a soft foot on the brake. Any sudden movement on my part would cause the box to stop dead and, if Tommy managed to stay in it, he would sway violently.

When the box touched down in the bottom of the boat and the cables went slack I breathed a colossal sigh of relief. From Tommy's point of view it was the start of a very long ordeal before he got to hospital, had his broken leg set and felt a measure of comfort again.

Lawrence Johnstone had come off to take his place, willingly giving up his shore leave to help out. However this state of affairs could not last long. The routine had to be re-established and this meant that for the next seven months we had a succession of supernumeraries filling in for Tommy.

What followed on the rock was in one way the time of my life and in another way the most difficult. On every visit that I made to the rock I was acting principal keeper because, as it happened, I was the assistant who had been longest in the service. That was the way the service was run.

A number of factors made this awkward for me. The men who replaced Tommy were a succession of supernumeraries who had never been to Muckle Flugga before and none of them could keep a watch without a crash course in what to do. Some of them had no cooking experience and needed a lot of help in the kitchen.

It was also at time of radical change at the station. A helicopter pad was about to be built as well as a new engine room. At times we had perhaps six or seven workmen and artificers with us to be fed and looked after.

With all the extra men we needed extra stores and water and the boat was off almost every day. The rigging of the boat's mooring ropes and driving the winch were two more things Supers had to learn quickly. It was a challenging period and every time I went to bed I would spend a few minutes quietly thinking about the next day and anticipating the next set of problems. I found this worked very well because almost nothing that happened came out of the blue. Every problem was solved before it occurred. One problem that I had to give a lot of thought to was the water supply. It was a dry summer and the tanks that stored the rainwater were only one third full. The cistern and plumbing were stainless so salt water could be used but to get salt water to the tanks was easier said than done. We were over 200 feet above sea level and there was no way of pumping up water. It had to be lifted. The solution came when I spotted an old tank that had been used to slake lime in.

My idea was to lower it down on the Blondin wire, let it sink in the sea and then haul it up again. First I had to calculate the capacity of the tank to ensure that, filled with water, it did not overload the cable. The next problem was how to get it to sink, the first time we lowered it down it simply floated on its bottom. I bolted an iron bar on one side so that, when it was in the water, it capsized and sank. I also had to fix a pipe and a stopcock on the bottom so the water could be drained without the need to manhandle it. I was well pleased with my efforts and the saltwater went a long way to solving the water shortage.

To make room for the helicopter pad one of the 90-foot radio beacon masts had to be demolished. Bob Gray was the senior artificer in our area and in charge of this tricky job. It seemed easy enough on the face of it but it had to be felled in such a way that it did not fall over the cliff. There was a narrow corridor for it to fall in safely. Bob took time and care and did a perfect job. It was then cut up into manageable pieces for removal. The next operation was entirely new to me; working with a helicopter. Large quantities of cement were needed as well as sand and water and it was reckoned that the quickest, and indeed the only way, to transport it was by helicopter. The aircraft was a small Bolko machine that had a maximum payload of 112 lb which meant it took many days to get all the freight onto the rock. Other than giving weather reports each morning lightkeepers had little to do with this side of things. The contractor's men unhooked each cargo and no marshalling was needed. As soon as the helicopter pad was finished work began on the new engine room.

One of the supernumeraries we had during this period was an Irishman called Declan McLysaght. He proved to be great fun and a very capable lightkeeper. Although he was born in Athlone and was a citizen of the Irish republic he had served in the RAF and had trained in the use and repair of computers. He had been posted to America and had spent quite a lot of time there. After he left the RAF he went home to Ireland and joined the Irish army. He was stationed in Athlone, a garrison town, and had patrolled the Republic's side of the border. He had married a Scots girl who was a nurse and her career took her back to Scotland. They did not want to be apart so Declan had applied for a job as a lightkeeper and had been accepted. He was full of wisecracks and never short of an answer.

If he had a disagreement with anyone a favourite saying of his was: "You're as much use as half a scissors. Why don't you go halfway around the world?"

When asked why only halfway he would reply: "If you went any further you would be on the way back again!"

Once when I came on to the rock he told me that he had had a run in with the other principal, my opposite number. He had made a mistake. In changing over the generators he had stopped the generator on load and the whole station was plunged into darkness and everything stopped working.

It was Declan's view that he had been given a row, a schacking and a bollacking away beyond what was deserved for making a simple mistake.

"What did you say?" I asked him because I could not imagine him taking it lying down.

"Oi replied in moi broadest Oirish accent an Oi giv im an Oirish salute."

"How does that go?"

"Wit an Oirish salute," he said, "you don't put the hand up the head, you put the head down to the hand, an Oi said Sorr Oi'm not tick!"

In summer Muckle Flugga is teeming with birds and Declan was very interested in them. A tiny rock pipit built her nest close to the clifftop on the north-east side. Declan kept an eye on her. Indeed we all did. We saw the nest, then three eggs and eventually the minute chicks. The mother bird showed no fear of us. Maybe she knew we would not harm her. One evening Declan and I were looking down into the nest. The mother bird was away, no doubt looking for food. We saw her fly in and just as she was about to land in the nest a bonxie appeared from nowhere and gobbled her up, leaving the young ones by themselves in the nest. Declan was furious. His eyes flashed and I never, neither before nor since, saw anyone move so fast. He picked up a stone about the size of a tennis ball and hurled it at the bonxie, hitting it fair and square in the neck. The bonxie, in a flurry of feathers, tumbled down the cliff and we never saw it again. We never saw the chicks again either. The following morning they too were gone. They had probably made a meal for some other bird.

To have unexpected visitors at Muckle Flugga was a rare event but it did happen. One party was led by a lady called Sue Anderson. She was from Cambridge and her mission was to do a census of the seals that lived on and around the rock. She made me an offer I could not refuse. It was a beautiful summer day with the sea as smooth as glass and Sue intended to land on the Out Stack. Would I like to come? I did not have to be asked twice. I got myself ready and just as we were going out the door a radio message came in to say that the boat was coming off with an engineer. I could not go to the Out Stack. Instead I had to go to the landing and put out the ropes. I have always regretted that I missed this once-in-a-lifetime opportunity.

Other visitors came one dull, dismal Saturday night when the air was laden with drizzle. At the time we had no workmen on the rock. There was Tommy, John Henry and myself. It was around 8 pm. I was on watch and the other two were in bed catching up on sleep before their own watches. From where I was sitting in the living room I could see the outside door through a window. I was aware of a noise. At first I thought one of my mates had got up but slowly, very slowly, the outside opened and a figure was silhouetted against the dim light. It was neither Tommy nor John nor anyone else I knew. The hair rose on my neck, especially when this ghostly looking man crouched down, disappearing below the level of the window. It was an act of no little courage on my part but I got up from my chair and cautiously opened the door to look into a black face; black because of a long period without seeing soap and water. The stranger straightened up and then bent down again, this time to pick up a one litre, yellow labelled bottle of Watson's Rum. I then realised that the reason for his disappearance below the window was so that he could set down the bottle. I greeted him with a "hello" and he reached out to shake hands.

It turned out that he was from Whalsay. His name was Peter Henderson and at home he was known as Peter o' da Lea. He explained that he and his friend Johnnie Bruce were going around the islands shooting seals. I did not immediately tell him of my disapproval but instead invited him into the kitchen. I put on the kettle for tea but after he had been in the warmth for a while his close acquaintance with sealskins and blubber was very apparent. Not to put too fine a point on it, he stank to high heaven. I went through to tell Tommy and John that we had a visitor but they told me in stark, blunt terms to bugger off, and did I not know that they were trying to sleep?

Peter drank a cup of tea and ate a biscuit but before he left he poured out three generous nips of rum for the three of us. I reminded him that Muckle Flugga was a wildlife sanctuary and that if he had to shoot seals he should do it elsewhere. I watched him leave and his shipmate came on to the rock and I showed him around. When all was quiet I stowed the glasses of rum in a cupboard.

The following day, Sunday, it was commonplace for the man on the morning watch to give the other two a long lie. That, of course, was me. The other two never got up until the dinner, at 1pm, was nearly ready. Instead of the usual joking and cordiality there was an unwelcome tension in the air that I did not understand.

John Henry was pacing up and down and giving me some filthy looks. After a while he stopped, looked at me directly and said: "What du did dastreen wusna funny. Du waakened me oot o me soond sleep."

It was clear that Tommy was in full agreement. It was only then I realised that neither of them believed that we had had a visitor. I told them the whole story but it cut no ice with them and they said that I was never, ever to do anything like that again. I remembered then the glasses of rum. Both of them knew that there was no rum or any other alcohol on the rock so they did believe me and gave a kind of a grudging apology and the good humour and fun came back to the dinner table.

Chapter 39

The Final Stretch

TOMMY Budge's broken leg took seven months to heal. Even then he had a pronounced limp when he returned to work. I was delighted to have him back. Not only was he a friend that I enjoyed being with but he took up his duties as principal keeper and I felt a heavy weight lifted off my shoulders.

In the meantime we had another change of personnel. Jack Barclay had resigned and been replaced by David MacDonald. Jack had been appointed to Flugga a few months before I arrived from Cape Wrath so he was due a shift. The shift, when it came, was far from his liking. It was to Davaar, away down in South-west Scotland and he and his wife Winifred, who is from Unst, were too settled in Unst to go to a distant station.

David had been to the station as a Super so we knew him already and he knew the station so the change was quite smooth. David came from Golspie and was married with a family. He was a slim young man of medium height and black hair. One thing very noticeable about him was the fact that he had no front teeth. He had lost them in a very nasty and potentially fatal accident when he was working on an estate in Sutherland. It was at the time when there was a miner's strike and everyone worked a three-day week. Power cuts were frequent and firms and factories were trying to find ways of continuing work without the need for electricity.

David was with a team of men who worked in forestry. They were cutting up timber with a large circular saw. Normally the saw was powered by electricity but they had improvised and rigged a belt drive from a tractor. Somehow David had got caught in the belt and thrown on top of the saw. He sustained a horrible gash to his forearm all the way from elbow to wrist and was never to have full strength in that arm again. He had crashed down, head first, so hard on the saw bench that most of his teeth had been knocked out.

David was a keen photographer and an excellent darts player. We had a board on the wall of the radio room. Tommy and I played every afternoon. We were so much the same standard that when we went to play we had no idea who was going to win. Tommy was far more consistent than I and came out well on top over the piece. David was far better than either of us and was at a standard that he would go for three dart finishes that involved two trebles and a double. Of course he did not always get it but he was a great player. He was also good fun and proved to be another excellent rock mate.

By far the saddest thing that happened during this time was the death of John Henry Priest. It was during my shore leave that we heard that he was poorly and, on a trip to the shop, Margaret had seen the doctor going to his house at speed, but later in the day we heard the worst possible news. I was able to be at the funeral and at Muckle Flugga itself all work stopped, the generators were shut down for the duration of the funeral service and the lighthouse flag was flown at half-mast for the day. For me Muckle Flugga was never the same again. I missed him greatly. It was like some vital ingredient had been taken away and there was never the same fun or enjoyment.

But life went on and there was no let-up in the work on the rock. The new engine room was under construction and we had a swarm of workmen to feed and look after. Much of the steel and component parts were landed by helicopter. The landing area was small and, therefore, the pilot required someone to be a marshal. The pilot was alone in the helicopter and could see nothing that was directly below him. Tommy asked me to do the marshalling. I had never been trained and knew nothing about the hand signals except what I had seen in a leaflet. Tommy did not trust any of the workmen and did not want to do it himself.

None of us had much experience with helicopters but Tommy had been off with his broken leg so had never been at close quarters with a helicopter. I was not keen on the job and this was partly because I had had a scary experience with the same aircraft when Tommy was still ashore. The helicopter was due to come off one morning when it was blowing a severe gale, force 9, and I was sure that any flying to Muckle Flugga was out of the question. I was very surprised when a radio message came through to say that the helicopter was on its way. I put on warm clothes and went out to the helipad and, sure enough, the helicopter soon came into sight. It hovered above the pad for some considerable time before slowly getting near to touch down. I found out later that such was the updraft from the cliffs that the helicopter would not settle and that the pilot was doing something that was very risky indeed. He had put the rotor blades into reverse pitch and driven the aircraft down to land on the pad. But land it did, the door opened and the single passenger, Charlie, stepped out and went to the rear and opened the cargo doors to take out his tool kit and Wellington boots. At this very moment the pilot realised that he could not stay on the ground any longer. As well as being severe the wind was gusting and the helicopter was in serious danger of capsizing and blowing over the cliff. The pilot took the only option open to him, an emergency take-off.

The workman was experienced in travelling by chopper and aware of what was happening. He tried to close the cargo doors but never had time. The moment it left the ground the helicopter twisted and slewed and the port side skid caught Charlie in the side and lifted him off the ground to a height of about ten feet before he fell off and crashed back down on the helipad. He was unbelievably lucky. A few feet higher and he would have dropped over the cliff or been badly injured by the fall. As it was he had a very nasty bruise and maybe a broken rib but I felt that I had witnessed a near tragedy. Neither Charlie nor the pilot wanted this incident to be reported. They were aware that an unnecessary risk had been run and I believe a lesson had been learned.

To do this marshalling job I put on a bright yellow hat and a bright coloured waterproof jacket and stood on the roof of the paint store so the pilot could easily pick me out. As the day went on I became more confident and we had no mishaps. The following day we picked up where we left off and all the material was landed safely.

My first encounter with a helicopter had been a sad one. It came two years before when my father-in-law died. I loved Willie Barclay Henderson like my own father. His death was not entirely unexpected. He had been seriously ill for some time but when the bad news came it was, nonetheless, a shock. Permission to go ashore to the funeral was readily granted and

Jack Barclay, who was on shore leave, kindly agreed to come off and serve in my place while I was away. A boat trip was arranged for the day before the funeral but the wind got up to the point where no landing was possible.

I was ready to accept that I could not be at the funeral and be with Margaret and her mother, Barbara, at this sorrowful time. I tried to be philosophical and told myself that this was the fortunes of war, no more than I knew might happen when I joined the service. None of that helped my feelings on the day and I had told a tearful Margaret I could not be there.

Tommy Budge was on watch in the middle of the day and I was waiting to use the radio to tell HQ that we had told the boat's crew to stand down. Quite unexpectedly he said: "Do you mind if speak to them?"

Of course I told him to go ahead without any idea what he had in mind. I wandered out of the radio room. I wanted to be alone with my thoughts. When I was outside I heard Tommy knocking on the window and when I looked he signalled that I was to come back in.

By this time he had finished talking on the radio and told me, to my great surprise, that I was to make myself ready for the shore because the NLB was sending a helicopter from Aberdeen to take me home. I could not believe it but Tommy explained that he had called on the off-chance that the lighthouse helicopter might be in the area.

In fact it was in Aberdeen but was doing nothing else that day and was available. It arrived in due course, having picked up Jack Barclay on the links at Burrafirth. This was before the helipad had been built so it could not land but there was little enough wind so it hovered a few inches above the ground. Jack jumped out and I scrambled in.

Later John Henry said that when he was watching me get into the helicopter he wished he had had one of those electric prods that they used to put cattle into places that they did not want to go, like boats. In any event they landed me at Burrafirth where a taxi was waiting to take me to the ferry that crossed to Yell.

The following day saw a very large funeral company at the kirk and at the beautiful burial ground surrounding the ruin of the 12th century kirk, near to the loch and the lovely Sand of Breckon. I was not required to return to Muckle Flugga that day but made arrangements for the following day.

The family was, of course, grieving but there was a sense of relief that Willie's ordeal was at an end. He had been ill for a long time and was often aware of what was going on around him without being able to speak. During this time Margaret had spent a lot of time with her father and the strain had taken its toll and I was so pleased to be with her. Our daughter Elizabeth was only three at the time but she had sensed the sadness and the tension of the previous few weeks and every morning, without being told, she would go outside and bring in a bunch of wild flowers to lay on his bed. He could not speak but his eyes, full of tears, would thank her.

The night of the funeral Margaret and I reflected on recent events; not least the fact that I had made it to the funeral. We knew then and appreciated the fact that the Northern Lighthouse Board was the most considerate and compassionate employer. Sending a helicopter from Aberdeen would have cost them many thousands of pounds even then.

During my service I knew other acts of kindness and it always came as unexpected somehow. All dealing between HQ and lightkeepers was formal, seemingly aloof, cold even, but there was no denying the fact that they valued their employees and listened to any complaints and concerns with a sympathetic ear.

I was glad to be back on Muckle Flugga. I knew I was being a bit selfish but the rough humour and comradeship of Tommy and John Henry came as a most welcome change from all the well-meaning folk ashore with long faces and offering handshakes.

As I have said, all this happened two years earlier. This was now the spring of 1979 and Margaret and I were both very aware that our time at Muckle Flugga was nearing its end. It was time to make a crucially important decision about our future.

I loved my work as a lightkeeper and I loved Margaret in every way. She had been so supportive from the very start of our relationship. She had gained her Higher National Diploma from college but had had no opportunity to work away from the house. Without a single word of complaint she had contented herself as a housewife and a mother.

Now there was the opportunity for that to change, although it came out of misfortune. My father was sub-postmaster and postman in Gutcher, but he had lost his health. He suffered a heart attack and had to have major surgery. He was never a well man again but through sheer determination he was able to return to work. As a family we discussed the future. I had been at Muckle Flugga four years and a shift to another station could come anytime, sooner rather than later. Elizabeth had not only learned to sleep through the nights but the time for her to start school was drawing near. The time was right to leave Unst one way or the other.

My father was a quiet, reserved man but it was quite clear that it would please him, and indeed all our remaining parents, if we would leave the lighthouse service and come back to Yell to live. I did not want to leave my job. I felt comfortable in it. I felt like I was part of a large family. I was secure and to leave was to take a leap into the unknown despite that fact that I was, in effect, going home.

My father wanted us to inherit the house we had bought together as a family and step into the jobs he was doing for the Post Office. He and my mother had a tearoom that mainly catered for coach parties in the summer. He suggested that Margaret, with her catering skills, could develop this and all things considered we could enjoy a satisfactory income.

In the end we decided that I would resign from the lighthouse service if the Post Office would agree to employ me, succeeding my father. My father and I made a trip to Lerwick to see the head postmaster and Dad, speaking more assertively than ever I had heard him before in my life, first asked and then demanded that I be given the two jobs.

There was a bit of humming and hawing and muttering about advertising the positions but in the end, after sizing me up, they agreed I would be the new sub-postmaster and postman at Gutcher. My father was delighted and celebrated with large amounts of whisky. I got caught up in some measure in the euphoria but still hankered after my life as a lightkeeper.

I did not tell Tommy Budge at first but gradually the news got out and I sent in my resignation to take effect from 28th September, my father's 65th birthday. In the meantime life on the rock was as hectic as ever. Work on the new engine room was ongoing and this meant we had workmen at all times.

As it turned out I never saw the finished article. The new building was still under construction when I left. In fact the job took longer that it should because a different contractor had made the foundations and when the main contractors came to do the building they found that the walls did not fit the floor.

T L Arcus was involved in this job. They employed a few local men from Unst, among them a young lad called Nigel Stickle. Nigel was immediately popular with his workmates because of his good humour and willingness to work hard. He was also fond of a few pranks and one beautiful evening the men were sitting in the sun with their back against the wall of the building we called the smithy. One of them had stripped to the waist and was enjoying a cigarette when Nigel climbed on the roof of the smithy, tiptoed until he was directly above and poured a bucket of cold water on his head. The man came to his feet with a roar. He got such a shock that, for a horrible, moment, I thought that he was going to jump over the cliff. Nigel had to make himself scarce for the rest of the night and until he had been forgiven.

CHAPTER 40

LOOKING BACK

WHEN the weather was good in summer it had long been my habit to go down the steps to the sea. It was usually when I was on the 2am to 6am watch, ideally in the long Shetland twilight, da hümin. It would be wrong to describe this as a quiet moment because of the cacophony of the multitude of wildlife.

It was quiet in the sense that I was away from the noise of the generators and from any human company. I often wondered what some city folk would pay for this kind of peace and tranquillity, sitting alone in a beautiful place surrounded by seabirds – puffins, razorbills, guillemots and gulls – not to mention scores of seals.

Wildlife on Muckle Flugga seemed to have rare confidence and, certainly, paid little heed to me as I sat within a few feet of them. I often stayed there as long as my watchkeeping duties allowed and it gave me the opportunity to reflect, especially now that my time at Muckle Flugga was rapidly coming to an end.

I only spent one festive season on the rock and that New Year was memorable because of the big snowfall. The proximity of the sea normally keeps Muckle Flugga clear of snow and frost. This was the exception. On New Year's Eve I was on watch from 6pm to10 pm and told Tommy and John that I would continue until nearly midnight, allowing them extra time to rest.

I set about making a special supper to celebrate the New Year and part of my feast was a meat loaf baked in the oven. It was ready in plenty of time but I wanted it to be cold, so I carried it in a cloth and set it outside the porch door to cool. When I went to take it in again I could not find it because so much snow had fallen in the interval that it was completely out of sight. I poked around in the snow with a stick and eventually found it, none the worse for being under this white carpet. It was a most enjoyable night. We had a lovely meal. As well as the meat loaf we had roast pork, lamb with roast potatoes and vegetables and a dessert to follow.

It was a rare event to have any alcohol on the rock but because it was New Year we had a bottle and the three of us drank a toast to the New Year. We all wanted to talk to our families ashore and when we did that we discovered that Margaret and Thelma were spending New Year in a very unusual way.

The severe cold had frozen the water pipes at the reservoir with the result that no water was available from any of the taps. Aly Sinclair had rigged an electric boiler in what used to be the washhouse and everyone at the shore station was busy melting snow to provide fresh water for cooking and flushing toilets.

On those first few minutes of a new year the local radio station, Radio Shetland, was on air broadcasting messages between friends and talking to people who were working despite the holiday season. In charge at the radio station was our former boatman, Jonathan Wills. He was keen to talk to us so we were on air and able to wish a very public Happy New

Year to our families and friends. After all that excitement we took up our usual watches and the routine of the station was back to normal the following morning, New Year's Day or not.

When the daylight came up we saw a Muckle Flugga the like of which we had never seen before. Everything was covered by a foot of snow and the most important issue for us was that the steps down to the landing were covered as well. If there had been a need to go there it would have been very difficult and dangerous to use the steps. The engine that drove the winch was water cooled so we had a paraffin heater in beside it to prevent any danger of it freezing and bursting the radiator. The diesel oil in barrels in the court was not frozen solid but there was a thin skin of ice on the surface. It was by far the coldest spell any of us had experienced at the rock.

More and more memories came into my mind as I sat and thought about my time on this most northerly outpost of the British Isles. I still had the treasured letter that I received from Brian Johnston, the famous cricket commentator. I was, and still am, a big fan of cricket and of the radio programme *Test Match Special*. On Margaret's advice I had written in to claim that I was the most northerly listener in the British Isles. I did not expect any reaction but to my surprise and delight I heard Brian Johnston read out my letter on air and send me greetings. A few weeks later a letter came through the post written and signed by the great man himself.

Yet another memory was the trips to Petester to fetch strollers. This word stroller was code for lamb. The man who lived in Petester was Tammy Stickle and he supplied lamb for the Flugga freezers. I am not sure whether it was strictly legal but what I do know is that the meat was delicious.

The lightkeeper ashore was responsible for making sure that anything needed for the rock was obtained and taken to the Ness in time for the next relief. The routine was that we would phone Tammy and ask him for a lamb or sometimes two. We would tell him when the relief was due and he, in turn, would phone the shore station when he had them ready for collection.

Petester, where Tammy lived, was the most isolated house in Unst. It was situated on the west side of the very long Loch of Cliff and there was no road that went anywhere near it. It was a good twenty-minute walk from the road at the north end of the loch and exactly the same from the road in Balliasta in Baltasound. The path through the hill going to Petester sloped up on the way and there were two gullies with burns to cross. We always had white cotton bags to put the whole carcasses in and tied a thin rope from the corners so that it could be carried on the back. The house was so far away from any utilities that they had no mains water or electricity.

Mrs Stickle was disabled and confined to a wheelchair. This meant she could not go outside. Nonetheless she and Tammy were always kind, the kettle was always on the boil for tea and Tammy would fetch a bottle of his powerful home brew, a brew that had stood and matured until it was crystal clear. There was a temptation to assume that it was innocuous, but omnipotent was a more apt description.

Another high point in the lighthouse year was families day. A visit by wives and children was sanctioned by the NLB once every summer. It was always on a Sunday and only if the weather and the landing were perfect. Some summers it never happened for different reasons but the weather always had a big say. I well remember one such day when Elizabeth was about eighteen months old and still needing a sleep in the afternoon. She could have slept in my bed of course but we thought that if she wakened and found herself in a strange place she might fall out of bed trying to get up in a hurry. To make sure this did not happen we pulled a drawer from under a bed and she slept in that snug and cosy.

With the memory of Tommy's broken leg still fresh in my mind I thought back to my own injuries sustained on Flugga. I had a badly burnt hand when we were burning old oil on a windy day. A squall came from an unexpected direction and set fire to the bucket I was carrying. The entire back of my right hand was one massive blister right to the point of every finger. On another occasion I slipped on a wet floor and twisted my knee. The relief was the following day so there was no dramatic rescue but it took a long time to heal and I was off work for three months, much of that time hobbling around with the aid of a stick. During that time came annual inspection day and I was at a loss to know what I should be doing. I was off work, walking wounded, but had to decide whether I should ignore the whole thing or put the best foot forward, so to speak, and meet the superintendent. In the end I decided on the latter and hobbled down to the boatshed where the boatman and crew had gathered.

The first man that I spoke to there was Bertie Mathieson, who put me under severe scrutiny.

"Lowrie," he said. "Dus med a rang mistake. Dus no polished dy staff!"

I had to make an effort to break the train of pleasant thought. I had to leave the birds and seals and make my way back up to the business bit of the station and do my watchkeeping rounds of checking the generators and the radio beacon.

It was my last spell on the rock, a place that was so familiar that I felt that I knew every hole and corner and every single component part of the station. It was now late summer and the relief was due in three days and I would be going ashore for the last time. Everyone around me was a friend, including the men working for T L Arcus.

I was sad to be leaving despite the fact that a new and exciting career awaited me. I especially looked forward to Margaret and I developing the café and the post office work I knew so I had no worries on that score. Nonetheless being a lightkeeper had been the best period of my life. I took to it like a duck to water. There was no turning back and it made no sense to stay in the face of shifting and redundancy.

I wanted my last night on Muckle Flugga to be special so I spoke to Margaret on the radio and asked her to get a bottle of whisky and two dozen cans of beer. This she did and it came off in the boat. I never told anyone that I had booze. I wanted it to be a surprise. What I did do was to speak to Geordie Johnson, the T L Arcus foreman. I asked him if he would stop work a bit earlier than usual. Normally they worked late every evening to get the job done as quickly as possible. Geordie readily agreed to do this and we had food cooked, cold meat and the like to have with the dram.

When Nigel heard we were having a party he asked if we could play 500, his favourite card game. I said yes, of course.

All the men, Geordie himself, Nigel, Billy Bruce, Alistair Wishart and Gerry Grogan came in from work. They all had a shower, put on clean clothes, filed into the kitchen and each of them set a bottle on the table.